NOW!

NOW!

BY REV. M. RAYMOND, O.C.S.O.

THE BRUCE PUBLISHING COMPANY

Milwaukee

NIHIL OBSTAT:

FR. M. SHANE REGAN, O.C.S.O.
FR. M. GABRIEL O'CONNELL, O.C.S.O.

IMPRIMI POTEST:

FR. M. GABRIEL SORTAIS, O.C.S.O.
Abbot General, Rome

NIHIL OBSTAT:

JOHN F. MURPHY, S.T.D.
Censor librorum

IMPRIMATUR:

✠ WILLIAM E. COUSINS
Archbishop of Milwaukee
January 12, 1961

In this book all quotations from *The New Testament* are those of the Kleist-Lilly translation.

Library of Congress Catalog Card Number: 61–9580

MADE IN THE UNITED STATES OF AMERICA

(3/62)

To GOD the FATHER . . . who by saying *FIAT*
. . . brought about CREATION

and

To MARY, the MOTHER of GOD the SON . . .
who by saying *FIAT* . . . brought about the INCARNATION

and

To that ONLY-BEGOTTEN Son of the FATHER . . .
who, by saying *FIAT* . . . brought about REDEMPTION

and

To GOD the HOLY SPIRIT . . . who, in answer to our *FIAT* . . .
will bring about our SANCTIFICATION

this effort to awaken all

ORDINARY MEN AND WOMEN

to the power and efficacy

of

FIAT

is lovingly and reverently dedicated;

and, after Them, to

Mr. and Mrs. Emmett J. Culligan and Family

OTHER BOOKS BY

REV. M. RAYMOND, O.C.S.O.

The Man Who Got Even With God

The Less Traveled Road

Three Religious Rebels

The Family That Overtook Christ

These Women Walked With God

Burnt Out Incense

Love Does Such Things

God, a Woman, and the Way

A New Way of the Cross

God Goes to Murderer's Row

This Is Your Tomorrow . . . and Today

The Trappists, the Reds, and You

You

INTRODUCTION

But there is no such being as an ordinary man or woman if by ordinary you mean what so many people mean: negligible.

Each human being is so tremendous that he or she merits a reverence that is really religious. For each is a creation of God; each a mirror of Divinity; each a feature or a facet on the Face of Christ; each an object of constant care and concern to the Trinity. There is nothing ordinary, in the sense that so many of us use that word, about any human being.

As for telling them what is the Will of God for them in their ordinary day — that is something that can be done only by God Himself. For He alone is cognizant of His plan for each individual, and He alone knows how each ordinary day fits into that eternal blueprint.

But if you desire another book telling them the necessity of their seeking to know and do that Divine Will every day of their lives, are you not desiring that coals be carried to Newcastle? Two centuries ago the Jesuit, Jean-Pierre de Caussade, gave the world a treatise *Abandonment to Divine Providence.* Who can count the works that have been issued since, with this treatise as their background and foundation? The Trappist-Cistercian, Right Reverend Dom Vital Lehodey, after World War I, published his Holy *Abandonment,* but did so with a deep deferential bow to Rodriguez, Drexelius, de Caussade, Monsignor Gay, Father Desurmont, SS. Francis de Sales and Alphonsus Liguori. Then, toward the end of World War II, Father Francis J. McGarrigle, S.J., in his book *My Father's Will,* gave us what can be considered a classic on the subject.

The earnest protest had got that far when the man who had requested this book broke in with a reiteration of his request; and gave even stronger accent on the word "ordinary." He was well acquainted with all the great works on the subject, but felt there was real need now for a restatement of it.

If anyone should know what the public wants, the one making the request was that man; for he was in constant contact with people. And if anyone should know what the public needs, that one is a priest of the Most High God; for he, too, is in constant contact with people. But . . . "Who has ever known the mind of the Lord?" asked St. Paul just after he had exclaimed: "How incomprehensible are his judgments and how unsearchable his ways!" (Rom. 11:33–34.)

The whole subject is a thorny one; yet it is one that must be grasped. For, upon its being understood and lived depends all man's happiness not only in time but for all eternity. In fact it is life, it is love; it is everything good, true, and beautiful. It is the very breath of man's being. It is the only truly important thing in existence — God's Will for you.

My petitioner has the correct idea. But one wonders if he realizes the many difficulties and dangers an author faces as he tries to clarify the matter and render it not only palatable but actually palpable for the average man who is unacquainted with the fine, forceful, and utterly essential distinctions that philosophers and theologians have to make as they talk on this subject. No priest of God would lead any child of God into fatalism. Yet that danger is there. No priest of God would lead a child of God into quietism or semiquietism. Yet that danger, too, is there. No priest of God would ever lead a child of God into any form of illuminism or pitiable and false mysticism. But how keep from doing that as you teach man to abandon himself to Divine Providence? The very word "abandon" sounds passive and seems to inculcate some sort of total surrender of human activity. The sound directive to "let God have a free hand in your life" is so easily distorted and so readily taken as advice to do nothing! On the other hand, when one points out that "nothing happens except by the Will of God," there are those sanguine souls, who, in a burst of false generosity, will want to go ahead and accept anything and everything under the misunderstanding that "whatever is, is right." No one faces Scylla and Charybdis more fully than he who tries to tell the average man what God's Will is for him and how to do it. Yet the middle course can be steered — and must be.

The whole doctrine is contained in a single word of four letters. It is the word which gave us God's own Word, and made it possible for every man to become a syllable in that only-begotten Word of God. It was pronounced by Mary at Nazareth, and it set in motion the ever immutable Trinity, as the power of the Most High overshadowed her — and "the Word was made flesh — and dwelt amongst us." That word was *Fiat.* It means more than the translations say; for it means ever so much more than "May God's Will be fulfilled *in me*"; it means "By God's grace His Will is going to be fulfilled *by me.*"

But while that word *Fiat* contains the whole doctrine, the doctrine is not expressed by any mere word. It is a doctrine that can be expressed only by a life. The two syllables can fall from our lips in a split second, but what they signify must go on and on until there are no more seconds to our lives — but only eternity. This doctrine *lived* is the only sure guarantee of the individual's development and realization of his genuine personality; for it is only when God inhabits man that man becomes the being God intended him to be. And God inhabits man the way He desires only when that man lives "in Christ Jesus" and acts as did Jesus Christ, "doing always the things that please the Father" — in other words, His holy Will. Since there is no other life that can truly be called life for man other than life in Jesus Christ, it is obvious that the more deeply the individual sinks himself into the Mystical Body, the more completely he becomes himself. But since Christ's life can be summed up in the one word *Fiat,* there is no other proper summation for the life of any Christian. "To be alive to God in Christ Jesus" (Rom. 6:11) is the only goal for any human in time or for eternity. So we must sharpen our sights on this doctrine of God's Will, or go through life without ever having lived.

But that is only saying that man should love — and very specifically that he should love God. To live is to love, and to love is to be ready to lay down one's life for the Beloved. Which does not mean that one is to die, but that one is to live forever doing the Will of the One he loves. That is the doctrine of Abandonment — and the doctrine of the Mystical Body of Christ for the individual man — be he considered "ordinary" or "extraordinary."

Ronald Knox, while still an Anglican, once said: "The highest form of prayer is acquiescence in the Will of God," which brings to mind François Mauriac's profound definition of prayer as "taking a direction"; and his observation that we men are not to pray so much as we are to "become a prayer." But the prayer of all prayers is the one taught us by God's only Son which begins with the words: "Our Father" and reaches its zenith in the petition "Thy Will be done — on earth as it is in Heaven." There, then, is the life of man outlined by the Maker of men. There is the whole truth this book tries to tell as it insists that now is the time to do God's Will.

One can be profound without being obscure, just as one can be popular in his presentation without being superficial or sentimental. One cannot write of God's Will without being profound. However, it is hoped that this writer in his presentation has enabled the men of today to realize what they most demand and need: peace; for as Dante said: *"In His Will* is our peace." Hence St. Francis de Sales could well say: "Do not look forward to what might happen tomorrow. The same loving Father, who cares for you today, will take care of you tomorrow and every other day."

But the one live question for living men is: Are we taking care of that "loving Father right now"? It is His Will that we should.

CONTENTS

NOW!

CHAPTER ONE

CAN YOU TELL TIME?

"I like your Christ," said Mahatma Gandhi, "but I dislike your Christians." He gave as his reason: "They are so unlike your Christ."

That statement has been labeled "unfair." But who would dare say it is utterly unfounded? We Christians have puzzled others besides Gandhi. We often completely bewilder ourselves. We know Christ to be God. We acclaim Him as "the Way, the Truth, and the Life." Yet, how frequently we go our own way, lead our own life, and trifle with – when we do not actually betray – truth? Now that is no mere apparent paradox. That is a vital – and can be a fatal – contradiction. Many explanations have been offered for this distressing dissimilarity; and some of them have actually been valid. Yet one wonders if the simplest, soundest, and most satisfying explanation does not lie in the fact that Jesus Christ could tell time and did so, while very few Christians either do, or can!

That sounds flippant, but it is the baldest fact. In his Gospel account St. John records that one of the earliest statements made by Jesus in His public life was: "My time has not yet come" (Jn. 2:5). That was at Cana of Galilee. The other three Evangelists tell us how Christ began the Last Supper which marked the close of that same public life. Mark says it was with the words: "The hour has struck" (14:41); Matthew, that it was with: "My time is close at hand" (26:17); Luke shows us just how keenly conscious of both the time and the hour Jesus was by setting down that soul-stirring line: "It has been my heart's desire to eat this paschal supper with you before I suffer. I tell you I shall not eat it again till it is fulfilled in the kingdom of God" (22:15, 16). How many Christians are like Christ? How many have you ever heard speaking of "their hour" or "their time"? Can you yourself stand before anyone and say: "My time has not yet come"; or assert with utter conviction: "The hour has struck," and have it mean that your life's work is about to be consummated? Until you can, you hardly merit the name of human, let alone that of Christian. That last assertion may seem to out-Gandhi Gandhi. But when we reflect on the fact that we human beings are creatures of time; live, move, have our very being in time; and that all our actions, as Frank Sheed once remarked, are "conditioned by time, rolled along by time, and all but drowned in time," then we come to see why he named this question of time one of "really passionate importance."

If we do not feel its importance, indeed, its passionate importance, we are but offering another proof that we neither know what time is, nor really how to tell it. For here is a commodity we squander with all the recklessness of a sailor squandering his money on a drunken shore leave; yet time is a commodity we are ever craving more of, and crying after like some half-starved beggar. "Give me time," cries the ambitious, "and I'll garner wealth, I'll achieve position, I'll win power!" "Give me time," begs the explorer, "and I'll really discover!" "Give me time," cry the artist and the author, "and I'll produce a masterpiece!" "Give me time," says the teacher, "and I'll develop intellects, I'll produce character!" "Give me time!" cry the students, the scientists, and the men of research. "Give us time," cry the sick, "and we shall get well!" "Give me time," pleads the dying wanton, "and I'll live aright!" "Give me time!" How that cry arises from eternity even as poignantly, and perhaps more so, than from time. What wouldn't Dives, the rich man in the Gospel, give for a moment of time; or that wealthy farmer to whom Christ said: "You fool! This very night your soul will be demanded from you" (Lk. 12:20)? What wouldn't many of the dead in the nearest graveyard give for a day, an hour, a split second of time? "Give me time!" Do we not say it ourselves? Yet, both they and we have all the time in the world! Actually! We have all the time in the world; for we have this present, ever pressing, ever passing moment — and in this world, that is all the time there is, or ever will be.

Gilbert K. Chesterton once suggested that we "stare at familiar things until they begin to look strange," promising if we did we would then "be seeing them for the first time." Surely there is nothing under the sun with which we are more familiar than this thing called "time"; yet, when we stare at it for a while, we suddenly awake to the fact that there is perhaps nothing in creation about which we know so little. Here is something as omnipresent as the air we breathe, yet something more elusive than the wind. We waste it with frightening prodigality, yet try to hoard it as misers hoard their gold. We find it as unstable as quicksilver, yet know it is more steadfast than the pyramids or the sphinx; we know it is as steady as the stars. We recognize it to be both as relentless as a tyrant and as resourceful as a lover. For what wound is there that time will not heal? what heart will it not soften? Yet what finality there is to this fluid and ever flowing thing! Once gone it is gone forever. Omar Khayyam wrote:

> The Bird of Time has but a little way
> To flutter — and the Bird is on the Wing.

And

> The Moving Finger writes; and, having writ,
> Moves on: nor all your Piety nor Wit
> Shall lure it back to cancel half a Line,
> Nor all your Tears wash out a Word of it.

There is the terrifying thing about it: time is a tyrant. He comes quickly. He goes quickly. Once gone, he is gone forever. He is a totalitarian tyrant inasmuch as what he takes with him is fixed with all the fixity of God; it has become in some way eternal.

But time is also a treasure. Every speck of it is of infinite worth; for with its tiniest particle man can buy God. Any split second is wealth enough to purchase an eternity of bliss.

Not many of us ever stare so hard at time. How few of us ever see that no matter how pressed we may be for time, we always have enough of it to achieve man's only purpose for existence and life's one ultimate goal; for we have now — this present moment; and that is all the time in the world. To think otherwise is not only to blaspheme God but to show ourselves not only not Christian, but not even humanly mature.

When God makes an acorn, it is that, ultimately, it shall be an oak. When God made us creatures of time, endowing us with flesh and blood, intellect and free will, it was that, ultimately, we should achieve a definite character, become truly distinguished persons with distinguishable personalities, who in time, and through time, should attain a bliss-filled eternity. Since God is God, He gives the acorn time enough to become an oak, and each of us time enough to become what we actually are – *Christ.* And that time enough is this present moment – this passing now.

There – this present moment, this passing now – is the time you can truly call "your time," even though you may not call it "your hour." For, not only is this everflowing thing utterly irreversible, it is completely unpredictable. No man can promise himself time's next split second. Will you have time enough to finish this book? this page? this sentence? Will God grant you time enough?

Staring thus closely at time we suddenly realize that what many look upon as a bromide is really a bombshell; namely, the fact that "there is no time like the present." Indeed, no! For it is the only time God grants any of us. He does not give us years, months, days, or even hours. He grants us nothing but this truly, indivisible, yet immense and immeasurable, Now. This is "your time" – part of "your hour." So, *take your time!*

Stare at that familiar saying until it begins to look most strange. It is loaded with philosophy, theology, and the profoundest spirituality. Those three words constitute a directive which will not only insure one's sanity but will point the way to sanctity – man's only ultimate goal.

Why is it that our many mental institutions are overcrowded? People will not take their time. They do not live in the present! For are not all fears, phobias, crippling anxieties tied in with the future – a time that has not yet come – and may not? And are not deep depressions, melancholias, and foolish guilt complexes connected with the past – a time that has gone, and is gone forever – a time that cannot be changed even by God Almighty? These dementias most certainly bespeak some relation to the fact that those plagued with them have not been objective enough to stay in contact with the one great, gratuitous reality called *now.*

As for sanctity – why are the highways and byways of our world littered with unfinished saints; why is it that so few Christians actually radiate Christ; why is it that two thousand years after grace enough has been merited to sanctify ten thousand times ten thousand worlds, so few humans achieve that full human maturity which is called sainthood? There is one very telling answer: we do not take our time! We either live too much in a future which has not yet come — and may not; or dwell in a past which can never return; neglecting all the while "His hour" which is "our time" — the ever present now.

It was the sane, saintly, ruggedly individualistic Paul of Tarsus who told us the correct time when he wrote so dynamically to the Corinthians saying: "*Right now* is the acceptable time! *Right now* is the day of salvation!" (2 Cor. 6:2.) There is revelation for you. There is divine inspiration. Yet we go on talking of "tomorrow, and tomorrow, and tomorrow." This arrogant, blind and blasphemous stupidity has been admirably summed up in that axiom which tells that there is "no man so old that he does not think he will live another year." Another year! When no man can promise himself even this hour. The nine choirs of angels must weep over our human conceit which so shuts out reality. *Now* is the only time there is. *Now* is the only time we have. *Now,* strange as it may sound, is the only time we shall ever have. But do we know what time is?

It was Augustine of Hippo, one of the greatest minds in history, who said: "What is time? If no one asks me, I know; but if I want to explain it to a questioner, I do not know." That kind of honesty puzzles most people. The best way to get them to appreciate Augustine's honesty properly is to ask them to explain just what time is.

After the above admission, the soundly thinking saint went on to say: "This much I dare affirm I know: that if nothing passed, there would be no past time; if nothing were approaching, there would be no future time; if nothing were, there would be no present time."

We may immediately snort: "Obvious!" But Augustine will go on: "But the two times, past and future, how can they *be,* since the past is no more, and the future is not yet? On the other hand, if the present were always present and never flowed away into the past, it would not be time at all, but eternity. But if the present is time only because it flows away into the past, how can we say that it *is*? For it is, only because it will cease to be. Thus we can affirm that time *is*, only inasmuch as it tends toward not-being."

As you try to think that through, remember our original proposition was that we Christians do not know how to tell time. When you have thought the above through, you will conclude that very few persons can even tell what time is. We speak glibly enough about it, talking about a long time, a short time, the present, past, and future times. But St. Augustine makes us all pause and wonder if we really know just what we are talking about; for in one point in his inquiry into time he asked: "Are the present hundred years a long time?" Translate that into your own terms and think Augustine's thoughts.

Can the present century be called "a long time"? Before you answer, ask yourself if it can even be called "present"? We are now at a certain point in our century. That means that a certain number of years of this century no longer exist. They are gone forever. The remaining years do not, as yet, have being. Who knows whether they ever will or not? So the current year is the only year we can call "present." But can we say with any exactitude that we have even this year as present? Hardly; when by the month of May, four of the months that make up the year will already have ceased to be, while the seven subsequent months will still lie in the womb, with only a possibility of having existence. But of the current month, what can we claim to possess as present? Not the days that have passed. Not the days that are to come. But only this present day. And of that, how much is ours? Not the passing hour; for that is made up of sixty minutes, each of which has sixty flashing seconds. Of those, how many are ours? Only the one that is now flashing!

But we cannot stop even there in our probing. For Augustine goes on to say: "If we conceive of some point of time which cannot be divided even into the minutest parts of a moment, that is the only point that can be called present: and that point flees at such lightning speed from being future to being present, that it has no extent of duration at all. For if it were extended, it would be divisible into past and future. The present, then, has no length. Where, then, is there a time that can be called *long?"*

The future cannot be called long; for it has not yet come into being. The past cannot be called long; for it has already ceased to have being. The present "cries aloud, as we have just heard, that it cannot have length." Yet, we go on talking about "a long time." What are we talking about?

Before he went on to find out, Augustine did what we never do often enough. He prayed, saying: "O my God, aid me and direct me." Then he resumed his probe with: "Perhaps it might be said that there are not three times: past, present, and future, as we learned in boyhood, and as we have taught boys; but only the present, because the other two do not exist. . . . Perhaps it would be more correct to say: there is a present of things past, a present of things present, and a present of things future. For these three exist in the mind, and I find them nowhere else: the present of things past is memory, the present of things present is sight, the present of things future is expectation."

Brilliant as that certainly is, it is no final solution to our problem. For that would make all time nothing but a figment of the human mind. Augustine was too honest to stop there. He saw that time is measured, and had even asserted that it is measured in its passing. He returns to that fact now and probes it to its depths. "If you ask me how I know this (namely, that we measure time in its passing), my answer is," he says, "that I know it because we measure time, and we cannot measure what does not exist, and the past and future do not exist." Admire his honesty and persistency. He has just proved that the only point of time that actually exists is the *now,* that passing point which has no extension. Yet he knows that we measure time, and he knows we measure it by some duration, so he honestly, openly asks: "In what duration do we measure time while it is actually passing? In the future, from which it comes? — But what does not yet exist cannot be measured. In the present, then, by which it passes? — But that which has no space cannot be measured. In the past, to which it passes? — But what no longer exists cannot be measured."

This question was of such "passionate importance" to Augustine that here he cried out like one in despair: "O Lord my God, O good Father, for Christ's sake I beseech Thee, do not shut off these obscure familiar problems from my longing; do not shut them off and leave them impenetrable; but let them shine clear for me in the light of Thy mercy. . . . My mind burns to solve this complicated enigma. We are forever talking of time and of times. . . . They are the plainest and commonest of words, yet again they are profoundly obscure and their meaning still to be discovered."

Modern man is too self-sufficient to cry to God like that. Which, perhaps, is the basic reason for his inability to tell time.

Augustine knew that there is both motion and measure to this thing called time. But just what motion, and how is it measured? "I once heard a man say that time is simply the movement of the sun and moon and stars," writes the saint. "I did not agree. . . . Let no man tell me that the movement of the heavenly bodies is time: when at the prayer of a man the sun stood still that he might complete his victory in battle. The sun stood still, but time moved on. The battle was continued for the necessary length of time. . . . Time is not the movement of a body."

Again this humble and brilliant man turns to God and exclaims: "I confess to You, O Lord, that I still do not know what time is. . . . Does not my soul speak truly to You when I say that I can measure time? For so it is, O Lord my God, I measure it and I do not know what it is that I am measuring. I measure the movement of a body, using time to measure it by. Do I not then measure time itself? . . . That I measure time, I know. But I do not measure the future, for it is not yet; nor the present, for it is not extended in space; nor the past, which no longer exists. So what do I measure? Is it not time in passage but not past?"

It would seem that right here Augustine's patience grew thin. Seizing a line from a hymn which frequently forms part of every priest's Matin song: *Deus, Creator omnium* — "O God, Creator of everything" — he analyzed the length of the syllables. The long syllables took twice the time to pronounce as did the short. This was fact. But Augustine wanted to know how it was that he knew it to be fact. By the time he had measured them and found that some were twice as long as others, the sound of the syllables had died away. So what was he measuring — and by what? Not the syllables themselves, nor even their sound, but only something that remained in his memory after they had been sounded.

The saint concluded: "It is in you, O my mind, that I measure time. . . . What I measure is the impress produced in you by things as they pass, and abiding in you when they have passed: and it is present. I do not measure the things themselves whose passage produced the impress; it is the impress that I measure when I measure time. Thus either that is what time is, or I am not measuring time at all" (*Confessions,* Book XI, Frank Sheed's translation).*

So, according to Augustine, time is the measure of motion, and the measuring is done by the mind. That conclusion put him in harmony with Aristotle who centuries before had worked out the identical definition. Centuries later Aquinas was to adopt it and teach that time is the measure of motion according to before and after. That is what the sound philosophy of Scholasticism teaches today in opposition to the extremists, some of whom, like Kant, claim that time is purely subjective, an "inner form" with which we clothe the acts of the external senses. At the opposite extreme are those, like the ancient Greeks, who teach that time is completely objective, "a receptacle" in which all the events of the world are enclosed. Scholasticism teaches that there is an objective element to time — motion, and, very precisely, local motion; but then insists that this is not time itself, for before we ever have time we must add the subjective element — measure, and, very precisely, measurement by the mind. Time, then, is no pure figment of man's mind; it has a foundation in objective reality. It is what the Schoolmen call an *ens rationis cum fundamento in re.*

That definition always precipitates the fascinating questions: "Is there time on a completely deserted island?" and "Would there be time in a city that was completely depopulated?" By now you should have been made cautious enough not to hazard any answer to questions on time until you have carefully examined all their connotations. The sun would rise, pass over, and set beyond this island and that city; but would there be a solar day in them? If you agree with Aristotle, Aquinas, and the Scholastics of today, you will have to say: "No." For you are one with those ancient Greeks who so wisely insisted that "Where there is no mind, there is no time."

Unquestionably, the telling of time rests with man. Equally unquestionable is the fact that the time to be told comes from God. For all motion, ultimately, comes from that Unmoved Prime Mover, whom we worship; all change is traced back, finally, to Him who is alone changeless; since every created being owes its existence, in the last analysis, to the only uncreated Being whom we call God. All time, then, is from the only timeless One. And, like everything else that comes from Him, every split second of it must have an infinitely wise purpose for its existence. Until we know what that purpose is, we cannot call ourselves truly adult, really mature, or definitely Christian; for, as yet, we would not know how to *take our time!*

"Our time" is now – this *nunc fluens,* this ever passing moment. That is all the time we have. That is all the time we are ever going to have. So we must seize now; for time waits for no man. No matter what your joy or your sorrow, time moves on. It is tyrannically relentless. Never comes a moment in which you will not grow older; nor will one ever pass without it bringing you closer to the judgment seat of God. Stars may fall, suns burn out, seas dry up, the very Son of God die – yet time moves on. And with what finality! Years ago a popular song was always pleading "Turn back the universe, and give me yesterday!" But no man can turn back the clock of time one ticking second. That is what frightens the thinking man: time flashes by; and each flashing second lights as its backdrop eternity! The *nunc fluens* – this present, passing moment bespeaks an intimate and inestimable relation to that *nunc permanens* – which is timelessness and eternity. Both of those *nuncs* belong to God. He gives the first, the flowing one, to man that, with it, man may purchase the one that never passes.

Now we are at the heart of this matter; for now we are at grips with Reality. Now we are in a position to reach Christian maturity; for it is now that we can appreciate that adult, mature, and most Christian dictum of St. Augustine: *Quod aeternum non est, nihil est!* – "What is not eternal, is nothing!"

That is where the consideration of time led this saint. That is where it should lead you. For time and eternity are more closely related than echo and sound. Every tick of time comes from Him who is timeless. But, since God is changeless, there must be identity of purpose in His *nunc fluens* and His *nunc permanens*. There is! It is *your happiness*. God made you to be happy in time as well as in eternity. But neither you, nor Gabriel, Michael, or Raphael; neither Seraph, Cherub, Virtue, Throne, Domination, Principality, or Power; not even the Immaculate Mother of God herself can be happy in eternity unless she and they are doing the Will of God. So, also, no man on earth can be genuinely happy unless he takes "his time" and does with it what God desires. "Your time" is "God's time." He gives it to you that, like Christ, with it, through it, and in it, you may help Omnipotence discharge one of His eternal decrees. You have this passing *now* of time that you may help God carry out part of that Plan He drew up in the "unbeginning of endlessness and eternity." "The hour has struck" for you to assist the Infinite in the governance of the universe. Once you realize that, you can truly tell time.

CHAPTER TWO

BE YOURSELF . . .
NOW
. . . AND YOU'LL BE LIKE GOD!

If Augustine, by his close reasoning, has shaken our complacency, we ought to thank him. For one dementia not mentioned in the past chapter, but one that is highly contagious, and has already assumed epidemic proportions all over the inhabited globe, is man's blasphemous self-sufficiency. One obvious symptom of the disease is the individual's smug self-complacency. To have that shaken even the tiniest bit is a great blessing; for we can thus be alerted to the two ways of being ourselves: the wrong way — and the right way.

Chesterton tells about being in a London pub having his usual jolly time with the group that is typical of such a place when in walked a man whose mere presence changed the entire atmosphere. Almost all talk ceased. Chesterton was puzzled by the change; for on the surface the fellow seemed decent enough. As soon as the man had left one of the regulars tossed his head in the direction the fellow had gone and said: " 'E thinks 'e's Gawd Almighty."

Such people are not loved. But who is there today who has not thought, or who does not think, " 'E's Gawd Almighty"? That is the dementia mentioned above — a disease that attacks us all. Right now it is spreading over the world like wildfire; and science is the breeder of the germ. For once it had given us the radio we soon plumed ourselves as proud possessors of a second Pentecost and a veritable gift of tongues. Then came the airplane with which we almost annihilated space. Today with man-made satellites, we are shrinking outer space, and swagger about as if we were endowed with some kind of omnipresence. Nuclear fission has given us the intoxicating feeling of omnipotence. To complete our "deification" television brings us a spurious, specious, but very seductive sense of being omniscient. Let us face facts. We are complacent. We do act as if we were self-sufficient. Subconsciously at least we think we are "Gawd Almighty."

Of course we resent such a charge. But we are now, remember, staring at familiar things until they begin to look strange. Let us stare at ourselves a moment. Today when two men "go up to the Temple to pray," does either stay behind to beat his breast and tell the real truth? Our world is not filled with publicans; for most of us have been too true to our spiritual heredity. We are all children of that woman who listened to Satan who told her she would "be as God" and of that man who ate out of that woman's hand. It is not surprising, then, that we try to be "like unto God." That was the primeval temptation for which not only the first man, but, in him, mankind fell. In ultimate analysis, it is the only temptation man ever faces; and the only one for which he falls. For what is every robber, murderer, fornicator, slanderer; what is every sinner, but an individual human trying to be "as God"?

This tendency is in our very being. It remains there even after our baptism. It is by a necessity of our very nature that we try to be "like unto God." The tragedy is that we make the right try, but, too often, in the wrong way. So it is a blessing to have someone come along and shake our complacency. There is then a possibility of conversion. We may turn around and do it the right way.

When the famed French flyer, Antoine de Saint-Exupery, was forced down by engine trouble and landed in the Sahara, a thousand miles and more from all human aid, and was faced with the task of fixing that engine before his water gave out or dying there of thirst, he did not go into his subconscious or his unconscious, as so many of our learned ones speak of things today; he went into what he called his superconsciousness and held converse with his own soul. This he later set down in a gentle satire which he titled *The Little Prince*. One passage reads: "I know a planet where there is a certain red-faced gentleman. He has never smelled a flower; he has never looked at a star; he has never loved anyone; he has never done anything in his life but add up figures; and all day he says over and over: 'I am busy with matters of consequence' and this makes him swell up with pride, but he is no man – he is a mushroom."

That red-faced man (isn't he you? isn't he me?) thought " 'E was Gawd Almighty," for he was "busy with matters of consequence."

Out there in the great desert, fixing that engine, with one eye on his vanishing water, Saint-Exupery came face to face with himself – and his God. The lonely winds that blew across the lonelier sands opened his eyes to familiar things and he saw how strange they are. "Where I live," he wrote, "everything is so small. . . . The thing that is important is the thing that is not seen. All men have the stars; but they are not the same thing for all people. For some who are travelers the stars are guides. For others, they are no more than little lights in the sky. For others who are scholars they are problems. . . . For all these, stars are silent." Then he turns to his superconsciousness, his soul, his real self, and he says: "You will have stars that can laugh."

One of the bravest flyers of our day had seen himself, his earth, his soul, and came to hear what all the great ones of God have heard since the beginning of time – the ceaseless music of the spheres. We can hear the laughter and the singing of the stars, we can become "like unto God," if we shake off our stupid self-complacency and stare at things until we see. In this day of apocalyptic changes, the one change we lack and very imperiously need is the change of the Apocalypse; the one that says: "God's dwelling place is among men . . ." (Apoc. 21:3).

There is One who is actually omnipresent, omnipotent, and omniscient. But our science (and many of our scientists) knows little of Him. We shall now stare at One who is too strange to us, and we will keep on staring until He looks much more familiar. We will stare at God.

Romano Guardini has accused us of stealing from words their real meaning and reducing them to so "thin a tinkle of sound" that they have little more than a "surface existence." They signify for us but they never reveal. "We are too superficial," he says, "to be distressed with the loss of meaning, though we are more and more glib about the surface sense" we still allow words to have. Stare at the way we use the name of "God." Does it reveal Him to us? Does it really signify for us? To the Jews of old it revealed so much that they would never even utter His name. They substituted "Lord" for it. But we – we have not the same perception of the immediacy of God, His greatness, His transcendence, His power.

The Jews of old knew God to be "He who is." That was the name that had been revealed to Moses, and by him to the Chosen People. That name did more than signify to the Jews; it revealed God's very nature to them. They knew Him to be the only self-sufficient One, He who is Being in Itself, the Source of all other being and power. They trembled before that name even as they had trembled before God Himself on Sinai. But we – can we so much as prove to ourselves that *He who is* exists?

Sad that we have to make such an "Irish bull" as to say that we must prove that He who is Existence exists, and have it be anything but Irish, let alone an Irish bull. But the fact is that Guardini is right: we have robbed words of their vitality. They no longer live and bite fiercely into our consciousness. They no longer shock us. They do not startle us into a recognition of reality.

The baby sciences of psychiatry and depth psychology, which have been so warmly cuddled by countless moderns, try to tell us much about our drives. They enjoy some slight measure of very superficial success. But in their attempts to alert us to reality they fail miserably simply because they know so little about those deepest drives which, ultimately, are behind our every effort and activity: those innate, ineradicable drives toward Truth, Life, and Love – a trinity, which, when examined closely, is found to spell God. For it is from the Eternal Trinity of Father, Son, and Holy Spirit that all Truth comes, in whom all Life originates, and to be with whom is deathless Love.

Pascal is credited with having said there are "only two kinds of reasonable people: those who love God with all their hearts because they have found Him, and those who search for Him with all their hearts, that they may love Him." We ordinary men are reasonable. We want God with all our hearts, with all our souls, with all our strength. Of course we do not always recognize our need, the nature of our desire, or the direction of our drive. But the fact is that we are miserable without the Infinite. Some of us may not always be aware that we are in misery, while others of us, who are aware, may not know precisely why. But the truth about every man, be he labeled ordinary or extraordinary, is that he is a king walking in exile, who can never know happiness until he has regained his kingdom. That kingdom is the Kingdom of God — and we will be happy only when we awake and realize with the whole force of our being that the kingdom of God is within us! Since God made us to possess that kingdom not only in the everlasting *now* of eternity, but also in the ever passing *now* of time, it is imperative that we know just what time we have, and what we are to do with it.

God is a usurer. He demands interest on His loans. Christ Himself, "true God of true God," told us this when He told of the king and the talents he entrusted to his servants. We have Gospel foundation for naming God a usurer. But we can never call Him a miser. He would never dower us with drives that have us ever questing after Truth, Life, and Love, only to frustrate us. He has placed us in exile. But His earth is anything but a desert shimmering with mirages. Truth can be found now. Life can be lived to the hilt — and over that hilt — now. Love can be given in lavish prodigality — and received in like measure — *now.* All we have to do is find God. And the search is not difficult. We will meet Him face to face if we will be adult enough to do what must be done, as Frank Sheed says, if we would show ourselves mature: "accept reality, cooperate with reality, not kick against reality, remembering that the reality we are to accept and cooperate with is the vast framework of reality which, by God's will, is what it is."

Reality is another commonplace word now. But if ever Guardini's charge was substantiated beyond all possibility of denial, here it is. What a "thin tinkle of sound" there is to that word on their lips. What a "surface existence" it is allowed. Contrast their concept of reality with Russell Wilbur's who writes, in *Essays and Verses:**

> Reality — if one has the courage to scrutinize it without rose-colored glasses and to smell it without previously sprinkling it with rose-water — is grim and terrible.
>
> "Our God is a consuming fire, a jealous God."

* Sheed and Ward, 1940.

> "It is a terrible thing to fall into the hands of the living God" — and we fell into His hands when we were born, or rather when we were first conceived in the womb.
>
> Reality is often grim and terrible even on its surface; it is always grim and terrible underneath the surface, and until we penetrate to its innermost core. At its innermost core, however, Reality is infinitely tender, infinitely strong to sustain, to console, even permanently to delight and enrapture the heart of man.
>
> Only heroism can penetrate to the innermost core of Reality — only heroism fused with humility. . . .

Do you wonder what this reality can be? Russell Wilbur tells you it is found by those

> who learn to make the right response to life in the deepest things of life . . . by those who discover within the depths of their own souls a Mysterious Presence . . . the Eternal Christ, the Comrade Perfect, the joy-bringing Bride and Bridegroom of the soul. And His name shall be Wonderful, Counselor, the mighty God, the Father of Eternity, the Prince of Peace.

What this priest of God is actually saying is that in every passing second, in every single event of our lives, many of which, on the surface, are grim and terrible, God Himself comes to us. Pierce the surface, plunge to the innermost core, and you will be face to face with Christ, the Prince of Peace.

Tall statements and large promises to make! Yet, if we are to make a kingdom of any sort out of our world, it will have to be the kingdom of God — and that is possible only in and through Jesus Christ. Pascal has phrased the truth differently, but it is no different truth that he gives when he says: "You will never approach happiness without approaching its source, which is God." Are we doing that, or are we deluding ourselves? Answer that question by facing a more piercing one: Does that word "God" merely symbolize, or does it actually reveal to us?

God exists. Only the fool, as King David said, denies that. We are not fools. But can we prove that God exists? After listening to Fulton Sheen prove the existence of God, Gladys Baker, one of his outstanding converts, thought she could have gone out and proved it to the Politburo. Her proof would have been sound. But it may be questioned whether it would have been accepted. For the Politburo was not then, is not now, and may never be made up of wise men. But the question remains: Can we prove that God exists?

Do not say what Gladys Baker said at first:* "There is no need to prove His existence. I believe." For as she learned, and as you should know, that is not enough. Adulthood, maturity, reality demand that this word "God" not only signify, but that it really reveal Him who is. We must know God. We must find God. We must, in a way, feel God. For God is no extra in our lives. His Will, which is Himself, is the sole reason for our existence: our coming into it, and our continuance in it. Frank Sheed was more exact than Gladys Baker when he remarked in *Theology and Sanity:* "Be wrong about God's Will and we are inescapably wrong about the reason for our existence. Be wrong about that, and what can we be right about?" So let us get squared away on this matter of proving the existence of God. It will teach us much about *now.*

We saw that movement is of time's essence. For a few moments (if God allows us that many) let us consider motion. As we look around we find that practically everything in existence is in some kind of motion. Living things, certainly; for they are always growing up or growing down. But also nonliving things. Not only things like cars that can be set in motion, but even such things as rocks, earth, and dead sticks. Erosion, or some process of deterioration, is going on. But who ever heard of anything moving that had not been set in motion by something?

To make this personal as well as practical, let us listen to the beat of our own hearts. There is motion for us. But none of us set our own hearts beating. Nor was it our parents, grandparents, or great-grandparents; not even our first parents. No. Your heart and my heart were set beating, ultimately, by Him who shaped the first human heart, then breathed into the man He had "formed from the slime of the earth the breath of life" (Gen. 2:7). The Great Prime Mover, who Himself is unmoved, set your heart and my heart beating. It is He who keeps them beating – and His name is God.

There is the argument as briefly put as anyone dare put it. The principle upon which it rests is: "Whatever is moved, is moved by another." There is nothing new about the principle or the proof.

* In *I Had to Know* (New York: Appleton, 1951).

Aquinas used it in the thirteenth century after Christ. Aristotle had used it at least four centuries before Christ. Adam could have used it in the first century of the world's existence had he been intent upon proving the existence of Him who gave all things their existence. But because the proof and principle are old, do not fall into that all too common fallacy of thinking they are, therefore, useless. Actually, each of them is as new as this morning's daybreak, and even as this present, passing moment; for each is utterly timeless — as must be every fundamental truth.

To keep us from ever again thinking we are "Gawd Almighty," it may be well to point out that this principle, which says that nothing moves itself, is based on one even more fundamental, a principle that is both deeper and more abstract, but one that brings thinking men face to face with God. It runs: "Everything that does not have the reason of its being within itself, must have that reason in another." You see how neatly that principle can be summed up in the one compound word: *self-sufficiency*. You must also see that if there is anything we can predicate about man, be he ordinary or most extraordinary, it is that he is *not* self-sufficient.

The argument leads us to the realization that if there is to be anything transient, there must be something permanent. We have to have hearts before we can have heartbeats; heads before headaches; faces before we can smile. If we have something that moves, it is only because there is Someone who does not move.

This is a proof that is swaggeringly independent inasmuch as it can begin from any kind of motion known to man and will always end with God. Take the motion of the electron around the proton within an invisible atom, or take that of the mighty earth around the mightier sun, the argument runs the same. It is as true of the ticking of the second hand on your tiny watch as it is of the waxing and waning of the moon or the surge of the seven seas. If there is something in motion, there must be a Prime Mover who is Himself unmoved.

When we say "something in motion" we mean, of course, "something in *being*"; for we are dealing with existence as an Existentialist never did. The motion of all motion is the transition from nonbeing to being; from potential existence to actual existence; from the mere possibility of becoming, to being in the here and now. Lest we ordinary men get to sound like pedants, let us sum up the whole thing by saying simply and briefly: "If anything exists, God exists." Should anyone demand a clarification, we will say: "If anything exists it had to *become,* i.e., be moved from non-existence into existence." The only One who could so move anything must have the reason for His own existence within Himself. He must be self-sufficient. He must be God.

We can keep it all personal, and make it quite pointed by saying: "I live. Therefore, there is a living God." There is nothing arrogant in that. Rather it is humble with the only true humility; for it is honesty and truth.

In this generation, which has been called "more pagan than that of Virgil," there will be those who will say: "When this universe was thought of as something tremendous from the very beginning, there may have been need for this Omnipotent Prime Mover of yours. But now that Evolution has shown that, more than likely, it came from some very small, primeval stuff, what need is there for this Omnipotent Creator?" The answer is simple – and devastating. We must have a cause for a spark just as well as for a universal conflagration. Size has nothing to do with our proof. If the original mass of our present universe was only the size of a subelectron, the principle that a thing moved needs a mover, that every effect must have a cause, that any existing being must have the reason for its existence in itself or in another, holds good. If it has it in itself, it is God. If it hasn't, it came into existence through God's action.

"But what if the world be eternal – what need then for a Maker who Himself is eternal?"

Never allow such seemingly profound objections to silence you. This proof from motion is so haughty that it can disregard the whole question of time and eternity. It really does not care whether the world was created in time (as Genesis certainly seems to indicate) or if it is eternal. It laughs at this would-be learned objection and says: "Just as you will never find a smile without a face, neither will you find motion without a mover." What difference does it make whether the motion be eternal or just in time? If you had an eternal face, you could have an eternal smile; but only on condition that there was a face to smile! If the universe is in eternal motion there must be an Eternal Mover.

The strength, power, and, one might say, the beauty of this proof will never be marred, let alone destroyed. Even scientists of the rank of Sir James Jeans are coming to recognize its magnificence. In his book *The Mysterious Universe,* Sir James had this to say: "Primitive cosmologies picture a creator working in space and time, forging sun, moon, and stars out of already existent raw material. Modern scientific theory compels us to think of the Creator as working outside time and space, which are parts of His creation, just as the artist is outside his canvas."*

Sir James is only saying in language of today what Aristotle said before Christ was born, and what every truly rational man will say until the Day of Doom. We must look for a First Cause who is Himself uncaused, and we must find Him if we are to account for the passage of a cloud across the sky, the movement of a leaf, the pulse in a baby's body, or the fire in Betelgeuse. The First Cause will be found standing outside creation; for the First Cause must be Himself uncaused.

That last line is answer to those who will ask: "If God made everything, who made God?" They are saying "Who gave being to Being? Who gave existence to Existence? Who caused the First Cause?" And that last form of the query gives us insight into the nature both of causes and of God. For so long as we ask who caused this cause, we are viewing this cause as an effect, and not as a cause. Our minds will go on seeking the cause of effects until it comes to that First Cause which is not an effect – but is uncaused and the Cause of every effect – God! So you see those who ask "Who caused the First Cause?" are asking nothing; for the First is first, or it is not the mind-satisfying explanation we are seeking; it is nothing.

To put it another way, let us say that each of us, as well as everything else in existence, received our being from another. That is evident enough; for none of us has the reason for his being within him; we are not self-sufficient. But who can conceive a whole

* New York: Macmillan, 1931, p. 141.

universe of things, each of which *received* existence? That is absurd! There has to be One Giver of existence who Himself does not receive; One who has existence by His very nature; *One who is*. Which, you see, recalls the description God gave of Himself to Moses: "I am who am."

What a difference that points up between God and ourselves! He *has* to be. That is His nature. It demands existence. God is One who simply cannot not-be. Whereas we — what a miracle it is that we *are* at all! What a continued miracle that we continue to be! We are so utterly un-self-sufficient that we cannot call the next breath or heartbeat our own. We are not at all sure that there will be a next. But God must always be. "I am who am."

When we have said God *is,* we have said all that there is to be said. But we are very far from knowing all we have actually said. Those two monosyllables contain all the truths theologians have been able to enucleate down the centuries — and all the philosophers will ever be able to know. For they contain that cascade of splendor which we call the "attributes" of God; for if His essence and existence are one, then He is infinite; for He is without limitation of any sort. But if He is without limitation of any sort, He must contain within Himself every perfection possible, and each in all its possible perfection. He is Omnipotence. He is Omniscience. He is Omnipresence. He is the Great Alone — alone in His oneness, His simplicity, His spirituality, His eternality. He alone is the Creator, the Conserver, the Concurrer in every act and action of His creatures. He, the lone Immutable, spins the earth, stirs the seas, guides the stars in their courses — and gives you and me each successive *now*.

All this we know from reason alone. It is not a question of feeling, sensing, or emoting. This is rationality at its most rational. This is closest contact with reality. It is staring at familiar things until we see them.

Ordinary men are capable of reaching these magnificent conclusions by use of reason alone; and, as we have just seen, it is a relatively easy process. But not all of us find the time to do such reasoning. Hence, while it is not too difficult to prove that God is not only Something — such as Prime Mover, First Cause, Source of all being — but Someone — a Person, not a mere Power; He who is, not That which is, still it will save time to go back to time's mid-most moment and meet Christ, the Son of God, and very God Himself, and learn from Him who God is, and what God does. The revelation He will make will not do away with our reasons or our need for reasoning. Rather it will force us to a deeper and more correct use of our reason, and keep our reasoning from going astray. But besides showing us God more clearly and quickly, Christ will teach us the practical lesson of what God expects us to do with the *now*. It will be a lesson in love-making; which is only another way of saying Christ will show us how to be ourselves!

We ordinary men must love. It is a veritable compulsion in our make-up. So long as we live we will know that compelling urge to give ourselves to someone or something in that chivalrous gesture we call loyalty or love. Now it is not easy to love a Prime Mover. It is not easy to feel passion for an Uncaused First Cause. It is not easy to cast yourself and all that you are and all that you have on the Source of all being. We are beings of sense. We live in bodies of flesh. We have eyes that want to see, ears that want to hear, lips that want to speak, arms that want to enfold. But our arms cannot enfold Pure Act. Our eyes cannot rest on Pure Spirit. Our ears cannot attune to the speech of Simplicity Itself. Nor can our hands ever feel the warm clasp of Eternity and Infinity. To know how near God is, to learn what real love is, to understand what life is all about, our reason has been given the aid of Revelation — a living Revelation. Now our eyes can look into the very eyes of God as we stare at the Child of Mary Immaculate. Our ears can hear God speak as we listen to the Wonder-Worker from Galilee. Our mortal hands can touch the hem of the garment God wears; they can take down and bury the very body in which God lived. Now we know God in and through Jesus Christ.

For that Revelation we can never be thankful enough. For while reason could teach us that we are more closely related to God than is the song to the one who is singing it; while reason alone could tell us that even now God is thinking us, willing us, working in us; that we are mirrors of God in whom His image and likeness will stay only so long as He stays holding these mirrors in being and putting His image and likeness there; yet it could not tell us that most intimate truth which can make our lives all good and beautiful. For while it could tell us that God is an infinitely intelligent Person, it could never tell us what Christ did: namely, that this infinitely intelligent Person is our *Father*.

It is magnificent to realize with Pascal that those silent stars up yonder are speaking aloud of God who guides them on their way. It is even more magnificent to realize with saints like Ignatius of Loyola and Paul of the Cross that God is in every flower, and to cry as did our own Tennyson: "On your knees, man, here are violets!" It is yet even more magnificent to realize with St. Paul that "God is not far from any of us; for in him we live and move and have our being" (Acts 17:28). But the most magnificent realization possible to mortal man is that this transcendent, immanent, infinite God is our *Father*.

That makes this tremendous universe anything but alien. It allows us to understand that vision Juliana of Norwich had in which she held in her hand "a little thing, the quantitie of a haselnutt . . . and it was round as a ball." Looking on it she wondered and asked within herself "What may this be?" and was answered: "It is all that is made." She marveled that it did not "fall to naught for litleness" and wondered how it might last. Then within her she heard: "It lasteth, and ever shall last: for God loveth it. . . ." She then looked more closely at this "little thing" and saw in it "three properties: the *first* is that God made it; the *second* is that God loveth it; and the *third* is that God keepeth it."*

When man-made satellites fall from their orbits or shoot beyond the moon, we can smile and think how our *Father* who made "this little thing," the universe, "loveth it and yet keepeth it." This is the truth that will make us free; for this is the truth that gives us the only real security. But it is a truth that holds demands. If God is our Father we must be His sons. Therefore, we must be like Christ. That is why we have said: "Be yourself – *now* – and you'll be like God."

Reason could put us in awe. But Revelation should put us in

* "XVI Revelations of Divine Love" by Dame Juliana of Norwich.

love. For while we haven't the faintest idea of what a Creator is or what a Creator does — since we never have, and never will, see something made out of nothing! — we know full well what a father is and what a father does. We have known the heart of a father, felt the hand of a father, shared the life and love of a father. So when we call God "our Father" we are saying more than all the philosophies of all time could ever teach us. Reason teaches the tremendousness of God; but Revelation tells of His intimacy. He is our *Father.*

In teaching us how to pray, Christ not only revealed God, He revealed the dignity, the duty, the destiny of man. Since God is our *Father,* we men are not only members of God's household, we are members of His family! And that not only shows the depth of insight John the Evangelist had when he defined God as Love — *Deus Caritas est* — but gives us the deepest insight in what a Christian should be.

How right Guardini was when he charged us with robbing words of their meaning! Think what the word *Christian* meant to St. Paul and the men of his times, and what it means to the men of ours. Then a Christian was a "new creation," a "new man" who lived "in Christ Jesus"; he was a man who could say as Paul said: "For me Christ is life." In those far-off days pagans had no difficulty recognizing Christians — they were so different from all the others. "Behold how these Christians love one another" was no mere rhetorical expression. Today how do we Christians stand out in any way from the pagans around us? Do we think different thoughts, use different business principles, have different social and recognizable moral standards, act in any pronouncedly different way from those who know not Christ?

The basic reason we are not like God *now* is that we have not been ourselves — our baptized selves — other Christs! We have not been sons of our Father, God Almighty. Perhaps it has been that we did not reflect enough on the fact that a Father is one who provides; hence our Father, since He is God, must be Providence. Consequently we did not realize that every new *now* is a gift from that paternal Love and fatherly Strength that stretches from end to end of this universe "mightily, and rules all sweetly." We did not appreciate the fact that this *now* is filled to the brim and overflowing with the Wisdom, the Love, the Life that is God. We did not know that what books call Divine Providence we can call, and should call, "*Father*." But now that we have been staring at familiar things until they look strange, and at strange things until they look ever so much more familiar, we know that we have all the time in the world, and, with it, we are to be ourselves and thus be like God. We know that God not only created the world and us, but that He cares for both *now.*

CHAPTER THREE

YOU ARE CAUSING ALMIGHTY GOD CONCERN... RIGHT NOW

"Confusion" is a word that has been given more than a "tinkle of sound" and allowed altogether too much surface for its existence in these past few years. Again it is thanks to the noisy baby sciences of psychiatry and depth psychology. But there is never an excuse for any real Christian to be confused. For him life and living may be hard, but they are never confusing; for he knows exactly what they are all about – God! And He is most simple.

If neurotics and psychotics are cured, it is only by finding themselves. Once they have done this, they have found God. For each of them can cry as did Augustine toward the end of his *Confessions*: "Late have I loved Thee! For behold Thou wert within me, and I outside. . . . Thou wert with me, and I was not with Thee." They should go on with this same ever realistic saint and say: "Thou didst breathe fragrance upon me, and I drew in my breath and now pant for Thee; I tasted Thee, and now hunger and thirst for Thee; Thou didst touch me, and I have burned for Thy peace" (X, 27).*

That can be called a description of a Christian. Baptism was God's breath, God's touch, and a very real taste of God. That is why we all burn for His peace. Creation itself can be called the breath, the touch, and the taste of God. Hence, all humans are burning for His peace. Dante has given us the prescription for

* Frank Sheed's translation.

that burning. It is found in what has been called "the most quoted line of the *Divina Comedia*": "In His Will is our peace."* Would that we could call it the line that had been most lived! There is the only place we will ever find our peace. But thank God His Will can be found in every place.

The "Obvious Invisible" is a very proper name for God – and for His Will. For His Will is Himself. But how blind we are to the obvious! To look God in the eye we have but to look at ourselves – or at anyone and anything else – and really see them and ourselves. For the Triune God is in us and in them in at least a threefold manner: by His wisdom, His goodness, and His power. God is thinking you *now;* God is willing you *now;* God is working in you *now.* This obvious fact has too long been invisible to most of us ordinary men.

It is said that when Michelangelo had finished his statue of Moses and, was standing back to survey his masterpiece, he found it so lifelike that he struck it on the knee and said: "Speak!" Of course it didn't. For while Michelangelo could "create" in the loose sense of that word, neither he nor any other human artist could or can create in the strict sense of the word. Only the Divine Artist can do that. But the point is that men of genius like Michelangelo, Raphael, Murillo, and El Greco could first think their "creations"; then, by hard, careful work, will them into being; finally, when finished, affix their name, walk off, and let their "creation" live on for posterity. The stone, which the statue was made of, as the canvas on which the artist puts his paint, would hold the new form the masters had placed there. But God cannot work that way. The original "stuff" out of which He made us and the universe won't stay – for it was and is *nothingness.* But like any artist, God first thought us, then willed us, then worked in us. We are the result – and the continuing result – of His thinking, His willing, His working. Were God to forget us for the slightest tick of time, we would cease to be. He must show divine concern for us not only from moment to moment, but throughout the immeasurability of each passing moment.

---

* *Paradiso,* 3, 85.

That all but inaudible heartbeat of yours speaks loudly and eloquently of the concern God is showing for you *now*. It tells of His presence within you by His wisdom, His power, His goodness. It says you are a breath of God and one that He is still breathing. We might as well look for sunshine without a sun, flame without any fire, as to look for life or being without God. You are because He is. What is true of you, is true of everything in the universe, and of the universe itself. So God is as near you as is heartbeat to your heart. He is even nearer. . . .

Standing at the rail of an incoming liner as it steamed up the Hudson, three French engineers studied New York's skyline as it stood silhouetted against a flaming dawn. The bold thrust of the Empire State Building's tower caught their eyes. "How magnificent!" exclaimed one. "How fearlessly executed!" exclaimed the second. "How faultlessly conceived!" said the third. The steps in their appreciation were just the opposite to those taken by the architects and the builders. For first that tower had to be conceived in a man's mind. Only after that could anyone have the courage to undertake its execution. It was only after such daring in thought and will that the magnificence of that thrust into the heavens could be seen. But once the work had been finished and the scaffolding removed, both architects and builders could go off to Europe, Asia, Africa, or Australia, and the tower would stand yearning to the skies here in America. For there was substance to the steel and concrete they used to build that tower. But what these men could do after achieving their work, God, the Architect and Builder of the universe, can never do, if it is to remain in existence. The Infinite Intelligence which so grandly conceived this world, the Infinite Will which executed that concept, and the Infinite Power which brought it into being must stay thinking, willing, working – for there was no substance to the "stuff" He used. Consequently God is within us and without us, above us and below us; God is all about us. If we but open our eyes we will see His wisdom, His goodness, and His power. If we do not find God it is not because He is too far away, but because He is too near! It most likely will be because we are too far away from ourselves – just as Augustine was for years.

How intricate is this body God has given us! How marvelous the descriptions of its functions in all their complexity! But one may as well try to describe the nervous system and omit the brain, or the circulatory system and omit the heart as to talk about you and omit all mention of God. He is your Center, your Source, your sole and incessantly working Sustainer. Were God not actually concerned about you and me right now, we would not be. But note well that this is no general concern on the part of God; it is as individual, particular, and unique as you yourself are. For from all eternity God has had in His Mind and Will a specific task for you to perform for which no one else in all creation is fitted as you are. Since He wants this eternal plan of His brought to perfection in time, He has you in His Mind and Will in a very particular manner, and literally, *has* to keep you there.

You have a vocation, a special vocation, one that is absolutely unique. It belongs to you and to you alone. No saint, no angel, not even the Queen of angels and saints, Mary Immaculate, can fulfill your vocation or fit into your place in God's plan. Hence, you are important to God. He has to have concern for you from moment to moment. Right now He is literally showering you with graces. Each is God's Will for you — and for nobody else. Each is an index of God's special concern for you *now*. But each grace given us is a challenge. For inestimable gift, though it is, it requires action on our part. Grace does not work automatically. Once we reach the age of reason, we can no longer be merely passive, merely recipients, as we were at baptism. Grace is a gift. But a gift is not something simply offered. A gift is something offered and *received*. Hence, you and I are not only under Divine Providence, not only parts of Divine Providence, but are meant to be "working parts." God made us to help Him run His universe, complete His plan for mankind, and bring to perfection His creation. Each of us has a specific part to play in the execution of His eternal decrees. That is why God shows such concern for us. He has to; for He is God.

On the north wall of the apse in the National Shrine of the Immaculate Conception in Washington, D. C., is one of the largest mosaics in the world, if not the very largest. It is that of "Christ in Majesty." The Polish-American artist, John de Rosen, who designed it, tells us how he went back to the Byzantine tradition of Christ the "Pantocrator" – "The Ruler of All" – for his inspiration. But this Eastern concept needed some modifications before it would speak to the peoples of the West. He found some in the eleventh-century churches of Europe. From his study of all these he finally felt he had what he wanted for our National Shrine. The majestic figure of Christ is forty-two feet high, full-bodied, young, and with face that is more compassionate than anything found in the Eastern Church. His outstretched arms embrace the universe, symbolized by the twelve signs of the Zodiac which can be seen on the arch above Christ's head. His hands show wounds – red mouths which speak eloquently of His love for us men. On His left arm is draped much of his rich red mantle reminiscent of that telling line in the prophecy of Isaias: "Why, then, is thy apparel red, and thy garments like theirs that tread in the winepress?" (Isa. 63:2.) His right arm, shoulder, and breast are bare – and clearly visible is that wound through which the soldier's spear found His heart. De Rosen tells us that the face of Christ links our mosaic with the earliest images of our Savior: "to the Good Shepherd of the Lateran museum, to the sarcophagi of the Vatican, to the apsidal Christ sitting in Glory in San Vitale, Ravenna." The cross of flame which spreads from Christ's halo may well be a reminder of the Last Judgment, when, as St. Matthew tells us, "the sign of the Son of Man will appear in the sky," and St. John Chrysostom assures us that "sign" is "the Cross, brighter than the sun."

But remember, this awe-inspiring figure of Christ is a mosaic. This colossal figure of our King is made up of tens of thousands of pieces of colored glass. Do you think that Dr. John de Rosen was unconcerned about any one piece of glass as the workmen set about executing his conception? Not after the thought, travel, study, research he had done before he finally put his concept into a fixed design. Each tiny piece, with its own specific color, had its definite place and definite purpose. Dr. de Rosen was most anxious of course that each fulfill that purpose by being set in its proper place. Do you think God less an artist than John de Rosen? Do you consider His universe less magnificent than this mosaic? Would you compare His Mind, His Will, His concept of beauty with Dr. de Rosen's?

Don't you see, then, why God has to have constant and continual concern for you? You have a place in His design. You, with your specific coloring of temperament, character, personality; you, with your definite shape and size, determined by your racial, social, economic status; you, with your individualistic shade of coloring, brought on by your particular environment, education, and experiences, fit one place — and only one — in God's world. Hence, His ever vigilant concern for you.

Think what it would mean to have just one piece of a mosaic out of place. Take, for example, the mosaic of Murillo's "Immaculate Conception," which stood so long in the crypt of the National Shrine. As you know, it was Pope Benedict XV who donated this work to us. Before his gift could be executed, Benedict died. But his successor, Pius XI, commissioned Count Muccioli, head of the Vatican mosaic works and workshops, to go to Madrid, copy the original which hangs there in the Prado Gallery, and put it in mosaic. It took the Count and five master artists five years to finish their task. Thirty-five thousand pieces had to be colored and cut, then carefully fitted in. So perfect is this work that many think they are looking on an oil painting when they view it. Now suppose Murillo could have been brought back to life to superintend that work. Do you think he would be unconcerned about one single shade in the coloring of those pieces?

You are more important to God than any stone to Murillo. You are a living stone in a mosaic that moves. You are set in the world not only lifelessly to reproduce beauty, but to radiate glory — the very glory of God. You are part of God's splendor which is to shine forth as long as you breathe. Master Artist that He is, He is constantly concerned about you. For mankind must form that living "Christ in Majesty" which Dr. de Rosen could but design for our National Shrine. We are not bits of mosaic in a representation of Christ Jesus; we are living members in that tremendous Reality which is Christ's Mystical Body. We must fit into His picture and His plan. The completed work must be more than majestic; it must be Infinite Magnificence and Divine Splendor. That is why we must come to understand what we mean by God's providence, and very especially as it regards each of us individually. For it is anything but impersonal! Actually it is the Father's concern for His only Son. That Father is our Father; for we live and are kept alive for one ultimate purpose: that we be members of Jesus Christ, that "through Him, with Him, and in Him" we give honor and glory to the all-glorious Trinity. Divine providence is as personal as your heartbeat — and much more important. In all actuality it is God's paternal concern about you in the *now*.

You will never know yourself nor your God; you will never know what divine providence is, nor what is the Will of God; you will never know what real life and actual living are, until there emerges from everything and everyone a "living Face" — that of Christ in majesty and love! You will never evaluate yourself aright until you see the eyes in that "living Face" looking with a love-filled concern on you.

Ours is a living God. Ours is a living Faith. But too often the truths of our Faith about God are allowed to be dead. Providence is a truth that throbs with love and life for each of us personally. Literally it enfolds us in a paternal embrace and keeps our tiny human hearts beating against the great Heart of God. Yet how do we think of it? How do we talk of it? How do we live under it?

If we speak of it at all, is it not like some dried-up stoic philosophers for whom concepts are about as alive as the mummies of Egypt? We'll tell of intrinsic and extrinsic finality found in everything from a bee to Betelgeuse, from a subelectron to the farthest galaxy. We'll talk of design and show it in everything from the crystals in a snowflake to the sweep of the seas. We'll prove that there is a Final Cause just as definitely as there is an Efficient Cause — and say that God is both. But in all this splendid logic where do we find a breathing Love? Yet Divine Providence is just that; for it is God; and John the Evangelist defined Him best when he said: "God is Love."

If we think of it at all, is our thinking not like that of some pale-faced, depersonalized scientists who live by slide rules, logarithms, and micrometers? We'll think of it in terms of light years, outer space, and the ever receding rim of our ever expanding universe. We may even use our imaginations as did Ronald Macfie in his book *Science Rediscovers God,* and say:

> Millions on millions of years of radiation were necessary to prepare such elements as carbon, nitrogen, hydrogen, sulphur, etc., which are required for protoplasm, and also to arrange them by volcano, cloud, river, and sea so as to render them available for man. Can we look on this tremendous preparation for millions of years — on the nebula, on the crashing suns, on the slow destruction of lucid atoms, all undoubtedly leading to life, without realizing the mystery of the protoplasm, without having a vision of the Mind behind the advent of Life?*

That may all be true. In its own way it is quite beautiful. But we ordinary men of today hardly know what a nebula is, have never seen suns crash, nor looked upon lucid atoms. Yet we live — and divine providence is the foremost truth by which we live. Hence, we long to learn how divine it is, and how truly providential for us personally. We are quite convinced that God will keep the sun in the heavens, the moon tugging at the tides of the sea, the stars in their courses. But what we have to be convinced about is God's concern for us *now*. Innately we are selfish. In many ways we are the sun of our own world. But since we have only one soul to save, one life in which to do it, one time to apply to the task, there is a salutary selfishness which we can employ to bring ourselves into real, vibrant, vital relation to God — or better, allow God, in His providence, to bring us into living contact with His ever pulsing love. Once we do that, we live. But how are we ordinary men to come to life?

The way we are to come in contact with God and come alive is, simply, a Person — a divine Person — who became Man that we men might become like unto God. If we would learn to live, we must study Jesus Christ; see how He lived; and pattern our way of living on Him.

That will be a beginning. But there is a more excellent way. It is to remember not only who Jesus Christ is and what He did, but to remember who we are and what we should be doing. Christ is our Model. True. But even more true: we are Christ's members. The two truths must be wedded — and bring forth offspring worthy of their sires: acts stamped deep with Christness. That will be not

---

* New York: Charles Scribner and Sons, 1930, p. 262.

only living under divine providence, but living *out* divine providence. It will be executing what God decreed from all eternity.

St. Thomas Aquinas tells us clearly what divine providence is when he states that it is the concept, pre-existing in the Divine Mind, of the order of all things to an end. It is the plan in the Mind of God according to which every least thing in the universe has within itself a specific purpose for its existence. An eye has been made to see, an ear to hear, a tongue to taste. And each thing in the universe is ordered to a higher or extrinsic purpose. Roots have their determined work to do: they are to extract chemicals from the ground. But they do this work for the nourishment of the plant. The leaves will take in other elements from the air. And this specific work will be ordered to a higher end: the fruit of the plant. But the plant, when full grown, will be used for the nourishment of animals. They, in turn, will nourish men. There is a hierarchy of beings in the world, and a clearly defined subordination of ends to one ultimate purpose. This our philosophers will call "finality." No matter where we look with intelligent eyes, we see finality. If we pursue our study until we find the Source of this order and the Designer of this purposefulness, we find God. He is the Mind who conceived this splendor. He is the Will who made it a reality which we cannot miss if we only stare at all familiar things until we see them.

St. Thomas Aquinas has defined it accurately. But St. Paul led us into the mystery of it and allowed us to see it in a "living Face" when he wrote to the Ephesians, saying:

> With this grace he [God the Father] has inundated us, by imparting to us all manner of wisdom and practical knowledge, making known to us, in keeping with his good pleasure, *the mystery of his will.* And this good pleasure he decreed to put into effect in Christ when the designated period of time had elapsed, namely to gather all creation both in heaven and on earth under one head, Christ (Eph. 1:8–10).

There is the Mind of God, and the Will of God. There is the design of creation – the ultimate of divine providence: the face of Christ! Did not Paul tell us this when addressing his Corinthians? And may not, must not, every man say of himself what Paul said:

"The God who said, 'Let light shine from the midst of darkness,' has shone in our hearts, to give enlightenment through the knowledge of God's glory, *glowing in the face of Christ*" (2 Cor. 4:6).

How often have we heard that we were made for the glory of God? How thoroughly have we been taught, and do we not know by that knowledge that comes to us from the inner core of our being, that we must do the Will of God? Then recall all we have been told about divine providence, and realize that we heartily believe all we have been told. Yet does it all not remain hazy and somehow unreal? There is no bite to the words when we hear them. There is no breath in the truths when they are told. The conclusions are undeniable. We admit that. But they are also dead. The living God alone can bring them to life; and He does so through His Apostle Paul. Listening to him we hear the heartbeat of the universe, and it is saying: "Christ! Christ! Christ!" Learning from him we come to know that "there is but one Lord, Jesus Christ, through whom all things have their being, especially ourselves" (1 Cor. 8:6). Being taught by him we come to understand "the unfathomable riches of Christ" and that "wonderful plan, that mystery which has been hidden from eternity in God" (Eph. 3:8, 9) "to gather all creation . . . under one head, Christ." Here is the man who tells us not only who we ordinary men are, but what we are to do. He says, "We are his [God's] handiwork, created in Christ Jesus in view of the good deeds which God prepared beforehand for us to practice" (Eph. 2:10).

Now we know what divine providence is for us. Now we see the plan of God for us. Now we understand the Will of God in our regard. And now we cannot doubt that God has a loving concern for us from moment to moment, and throughout the length, breadth, and depth of every moment. We are His only Son's living members. That is why we were born. That is why we came into this world. That is why we are kept in being. Christ is the one great Reality of all time. Christ is the one great Reality *now.* Christ is the only Reality ordinary men need bother about. For such is the Will of God.

God has spoken, and God yet speaks. Prophets have long been silent. Apostles are centuries dead. Yet modern man can hear the voice of God as clearly as did the Jews of old when Moses, Ezechiel, Isaias, or Daniel spoke. They can hear the voice of Christ as clearly as ever Simon Peter or the sons of Zebedee, as clearly as Saul of Tarsus. Christ commissioned His Apostles to teach and endowed them with His own authority. "Who hears you, hears me" (Lk. 10:16). Those Apostles have had and yet have successors. We have heard Christ speaking; and we shall yet hear Him. As our century opened we heard Christ, and Paul, as we heard St. Pius X tell his aim, to "renew all things in Christ." That same voice of God came to us again when Pius XI spoke of "the peace of Christ in the reign of Christ." As our century reached its halfway mark we all but saw Christ as we looked and listened to Pius XII. Through these many mouthpieces God has spoken as eloquently as He did through the prophets of old; and He has told us even more clearly that all creation is for Christ, and through Christ, and in Christ.

That is the truth which will simplify life and living, as it unifies our diverse strivings, gives oneness to the countless calls on our time and abilities, and integrates all that appears so hopelessly disjointed and fragmented. The Will of God is that we "become what we are." But we too seldom realize what we are. We think of ourselves as mere men, limited by time and space, seemingly with more liabilities than assets, weighed down by a body requiring constant care, thus stifling a spirit that would soar, and creating a tension of which we are keenly conscious but whose exact nature we have not plumbed. We feel harassed, uneasy, and even somewhat confused; for we are without center. What we want is given us in this truth about God's Will. For "in Christ Jesus" we can enjoy that mind-saving, soul-saving, heart-satisfying synthesis which will enable us to adhere to God with our whole being even as we energetically give ourselves to a life of wholesome productivity in the world we know. "In Christ Jesus" we can revitalize, elevate, unify every sphere of existence and every legitimate activity. To become what we are does not call for a withdrawal from the world of today or a cessation of human endeavor and productivity, rather it demands a deeper plunge into that world and a recognition of the real worth of man's works.

God wills that we be ourselves, but that is something we can never be until we have stopped living on the surface of ourselves and gone down deep into the reality of our being. There we meet more than ourselves. There we meet God—and His Christ!

It is both fascinating and encouraging to find men of science rediscovering God. Many of them are awakening to the realization that they never formulate the laws that they discover, but that those laws have been written into the very essences of the things with which they work. Some are even saying again what the wise English astronomer once said as he discovered a law: "O Lord God, I am thinking Your thoughts after You."

Sir James Jeans comes very near to saying just that when he speaks of matter and light. He says:

> Matter is bottled light; light, as we commonly understand it, is unbottled light. Free mass from its chains and it will release light. In the sun, for example, matter is dissolving into radiation at the rate of four million tons a second. Radiation is thus the fundamental stuff of which the universe is made. The dust we tramp under our feet and the star discovered only yesterday by the astronomer are linked together by the unity of light and the laws of radiation. Modern science has thus come back face to face with the mystery of creation, and is really not closer to that mystery than was Moses when he wrote: "God said: 'Let there be light and light was made.'"*

No scientist will ever be closer to the mystery, or to its solution, than was John the Evangelist when he wrote: "When time began the Word was there, and the Word was face to face with God, and the Word was God. The Word, when time began, was face to face with God. All things came into being through him, and without him there came to be not one thing that has come to be. In him was life, and the life was the light of men. The light shines in the darkness, and the darkness did not lay hold of it" (Jn. 1:1–5). Eight chapters later the same Evangelist writes: "Once more Jesus addressed them. He said: "I am the light of the world. He who follows me will not walk in the dark, but have the light of life" (Jn. 8:12). Again and again in His public life Jesus called Himself "the Light of the World" and even stated the reason why He came:

---

* *The Mysterious Universe* (New York: Macmillan, 1931).

"so that no one who believes in me might remain in darkness" (Jn. 12:46).

Is that the key to the confusion of our day? Is ours an age of darkness principally because of neglect of Christ? Must He still say of our day what He said to Nicodemus about his day: "The light has come into the world, but men loved the darkness more than the light, because their lives were bad. Only an evil doer hates the light and refuses to face the light, for fear his practices may be exposed; but one who lives up to the truth faces the light, so that everyone can see that his life is lived in union with God" (Jn. 3:19–21).

We live in union with God when we are doing the Will of God. So we need to examine our consciences concerning this question of light. For St. Matthew reports that, in the Sermon on the Mount, this Word of God, this only Son of God, this Second Person of the Blessed Trinity who called Himself Truth said: "You are the light of the world . . . so let your light shine before your fellow men, that they may see your good example and praise your Father who is in heaven" (Mt. 5:14–16).

If the world is in darkness is it not because we ordinary men have not been doing the Will of God? Christ is the Light of the World — we are His members! We, then, must be flames in that Light. He said He had come "to cast fire upon the earth" (Lk. 12:49). If our world is not ablaze, can it be because we have not been kindled? Can it be that we have been hiding our light?

When that Prime Mover first said *Fiat lux* He was thinking of Christ, who would be the "Light of the World" and the "Lamp" of the world to come; He was thinking of the glory that would come to the Trinity from this Light while in our world and of the Glory of God which would light up the Jerusalem that would be heaven. He was thinking of darkness, too: not only of that darkness which we call the "first creation," but of that deeper darkness men would make and which would have to be lighted by the Son of God; He was thinking of how this Son would kindle other lights in that darkness which would come finally to burn forever before that Source and Center of all light — that Throne whereon God sits in "Light Inaccessible." He was thinking of you then. He is thinking of you now. For He is intimately, deeply, and, as it were, anxiously concerned about His own glory. You were made to give Him that. You are kept in creation that "your light may shine before your fellow men, that they may see your good example and praise your Father who is in Heaven" (Mt. 5:14).

That brings you back to the truth that God is your Father; hence, providence is paternal love. That brings you back to that other truth which Juliana of Norwich saw so clearly: that the universe, in the eyes of your Father, is tiny – and lovable! Juliana was but being blessed with the vision Wisdom tells when it says: "All things thou lovest, nor holdest any of thy creatures in abhorrence; hate and create thou couldst not, nor does aught abide save at thy will, whose summoning word holds them in being. They are thine, and thou sparest them; all things that live thou lovest, thou, the Master of them all" (Wisd. 11:25–27). Those two verses hold volumes of theology, truth enough to break the heart, so tender do they show our God to be. They complement that other truth which is directed so positively to man's head: "Clay we are in the potter's hand; it is for him who made us to dispose of us; clay is what the potter wills it to be, and we are in our maker's hands" (Ecclus. 33:13, 14). True enough; but truer still is it that we are in our Maker's heart; for His Will and His wisdom are His love.

The love of God for you is such that He is far more concerned with your health and happiness than you could ever be. It was God's Own and Only Begotten who told you the very "hairs of your head are numbered" . . . and that you are "more precious" to God "than whole flocks of sparrows," "five of which are sold for two pennies" but "no one of them is a poor forgotten creature" (Lk. 12:6, 7). Not only are the hairs of your head numbered but so is your every breath numbered by God; for He has to be in every breath. God, the almighty, infinite, eternal, omniscient, immutable One is concerned this moment about your digestion or your indigestion, your headache and cold, or the absence of both, about the working of every single cell in your body. This concern comes not only from your nature, which is utterly dependent and requires this constant care by God, but also from His nature. For He is a Being who cannot act save for His own glory; He is not only a holy God, a mighty God, but also a jealous God. He tells us so again and again in His books of Revelation. "The Lord, his name is Jealous," says He in one place (Exod. 34:14), and in another: "I am the Lord thy God, mighty and Jealous" (Exod. 20:5). There is one thing He is jealous of — His glory. And that, Paul told us, is to be seen "glowing in the face of Christ" (2 Cor. 4:6). You, in all truth, are a feature in that face; for you are His member!

God the Father, to whom we attribute providence, is wholly concerned with, and entirely taken up in, His Word. It was that Word who became flesh. By baptism men are made "the flesh of Christ" as Pope St. Leo the Great taught and Pope Pius XII re-taught when the latter wrote his encyclical *Mystici Corporis*. So, far from spinning any fancy when we tell you that Almighty God is greatly concerned about you *now,* we are giving theology that is as deep as God, as true as God, and just as loving. Providence is personal. It means that God is not only watching over you right now, but working in you, trying to bring you to that brilliance which is the glory "glowing in the face of Christ"; striving to make life as simple and as loving as is the spirit behind that statement of Teresa of Avila: "Lord, Thou knowest all things, canst do all things, and Thou lovest me."

There is the basis for peace of soul, happiness of heart, and joy in living. Since God is our Father and is omnipotent, since He is the One of whom Mardochai spoke when he said: "O Lord, thou art the sovereign Lord and king of all things; nothing but is subject to thy power. Who then can withstand thy will? . . . Heaven and earth and all that heaven's vault contains is thy creation; thy dominion is universal, thy royalty unchallengeable" (Esther 13:10, 11), we can look out on a world in tumult and be without a shadow of fear. Though death rise up from the darkness of the sea; though destruction rain down on us from the skies; though it seem that the seven vials of God's wrath are being poured out upon our world, we can still be without any deep disturbance; for we know that God *is* God, and that "He, the Lord of the universe that made great and little alike, cares alike for all" and that His wisdom and love, which we call providence, is "bold in her sweep from world's end to world's end" (Wisd. 6:8; 8:1).

Staring at things until we see them, we come to understand what sounds like impatience on the part of Christ with us and our careful, shrewd, calculating concern about food and clothing.

> Do not fret [He commands] about what to eat, or what to drink to sustain your life, or about what to wear on your bodies. . . . Look at the birds of the air: they do not sow or reap, or store up provisions in barns, and yet your heavenly Father feeds them! Are you not more precious than they? And which of you by fretting can add one minute to his span of life? . . . What little Faith you have! Therefore, have done with fretting . . . your heavenly Father knows you need all these things . . . let your first concern be the kingdom of God and what he requires of you; then you will have these things thrown in for good measure (Mt. 6:25–34).

What does God require of you? That you do His Will. That you become who you are. He is ordering His universe *now* just to help you do that.

CHAPTER FOUR

FACING AN OBJECTION . . . NOW . . . GIVES GOD A "NEW LOOK"

Down in the depths of our being we know that God is; that He reaches from "end to end mightily and orders all things sweetly"; that divine providence is a fact, and that it must be paternal. But we also wonder why such truths seem so far removed from everyday reality. Where is God in this continual and wearying struggle for existence? Where is He in this battle to make ends meet? Where is He when the proverbial "wolf" is at the door, or the unproverbial doctor or undertaker?

Reason may force us to accept the proofs about creation, preservation, and providence. But grim realities seem to nullify or at least make those proofs impractical.

Thus it is easy enough to see God in a sunset over a smoothly undulating sea. But where is He in the tidal wave or those cruelly battering storms at sea? Looking on a landscape that is all gold, russet, yellow, and red, no one will blame the poet for saying: "Some of us call it Autumn; but others call it God." There are times when this earth of ours is sheer magnificence – and God is all but felt. But there are other times when this earth of ours quakes, and the land slides. Where then is our God?

It is easy enough to see God in the eyes of a class of First Communicants; in the eyes of pure young love; in the eyes of a modern madonna as she bends over her baby. But there are other human eyes in which lights flash that are anything but love lights; eyes that hold flames never kindled by angels or set rising by God.

To be practical, it has been easy enough for us of this century to see God in men like St. Pius X, Pius XI, Pius XII, and John XXIII; but where is God in men like Hitler, Stalin, and the commandants of such places as Dachau and Auschwitz? Were the purges and the crematories parts of His plan? Are we to see paternal love in everything – in plagues, pestilences, devastating droughts and deluges, famines, fires, and the horrors of totalitarianism and wars? Is that theology or blasphemy?

To take in the full sweep of the cosmic picture of this twentieth century makes one think along the lines of Omar Khayyam:

> Ah Love! could you and I with Him conspire
> To grasp this sorry scheme of things entire,
>   Would we not shatter it to bits – and then
> Remould it nearer to the Heart's Desire!

We had that money panic in the first decade; World War I in the second decade; Hitler in the third; World War II in the fourth; between those two world wars we had the world-wide depression; and since the close of World War II what have we had but the terrors of a cold war and the inhuman cruelties behind those iron and bamboo curtains. Is God to be seen here?

It will not do to turn metaphysical and use philosophical terminology to convince the seriously inquiring man. It will not do to say that evil is nothing, since it is always a "privation" or a "negation." Tuberculosis and cancer can both be designated as a "lack of health," a "privation" – but who will accept either as a mere "negation"? To the ordinary man a storm is more than a "lack" of calm weather. To him the wind and rain are too real. So is the devastation they cause. War is a lack of peace. True. But what are bombs, bullets, bacteria, and bayonets? No, to the ordinary man philosophical terms and truths are a bit too subtle. The privation or negation presses in on him with too much personal weight for him to think that they are nothing.

The honest man admits that his whole being throbs with that tantalizing question so often met with on the lips of the enemies of God's Chosen People: "Where now is your God?" When pain grips and sorrow is our only food, this doctrine of the universality of God's causation and God's care bristles with difficulties. Logically we admit the need of a "Designer Infinite" for the sun, the moon, the stars, and the sea; for the roll of our world around the sun. But psychologically we are stunned by hate in human hearts, devastation in human hands. Then we hear in our pulses the pounding of that ominous question: "Where now is your God?"

There is an answer to that question. Paul of Tarsus, a realist among realists, is the one God chose to reveal it. But we will never accept this bit of revelation unless we realize that emotion colors our thinking, innate selfishness makes us shortsighted. Despite the profound Pascal and his line about the "heart having reasons the mind knows not of," it still remains fact that when we think with our heads, we think; when we think with our hearts, we emote, we feel, and may even grow intellectually passionate. If God is Reality, then everything real comes from Him — and remains real only because of Him. If the specific reality happens to be painful and personally repulsive, neither its painfulness nor its repulsiveness changes the place of its origin or the cause of its continuance in reality. Reason will tell us that much. But Revelation tells us something deeper, more intimate, and ultimately much more consoling. Paul says: "He [Christ] is the image of the invisible God, the first-born of every creature, because in him were created all creatures. . . . All have been created through him and for him. He exists prior to all creatures, and in him they are all preserved in being" (Col. 1:15–17).

As the solution to every difficulty, no matter what its nature, God offers us Christ as our ultimate. Note that Paul says every creature has been created *by* Christ, *through* Christ, *for* Christ; and each is kept in being *in* Christ. That plan of God, which takes in creation, providence, and the Apocalypse, is of a piece. Staring at it, we see the face of Christ, who is God.

So be virile enough of intellect to accept the fact. God is in the H-bomb just as really as He is in the sun. God is in the fall-out after an atomic explosion just as really as He is in the silver splendor of Yosemite's Bridal Veil Falls. God is in the workings of carcinoma just as really as He is in the workings of human conception. Everything and anything that has any form of existence rests continually in the hands of Him who alone can give existence — God.

But now let us insert a distinction of paramount importance, without which we will never be able to grasp truth at all. It lies in the difference between actual volition and mere permission. But that difference, in the matter under concern, is as deep as God, and points to contrasts more striking than those between night and day; it points to opposites as far removed as heaven and hell. Perhaps it will help to state boldly that God does not *will* all that transpires. There is much going on in our world today that He merely *permits*. You may be able to clarify the situation for yourself by saying that God does not will what He simply permits. That last word was canonized in the strictest sense of the term by the Council of Trent back in the middle of the sixteenth century when the Council thundered an anathema toward anyone who would say "that it is not in man's power to make his ways evil, but that God performs the evil works just as He performs the good, not only *permissively* but also properly and directly, so that Judas' betrayal no less than Paul's vocation was God's own work."

God did knock Saul of Tarsus from his horse. But God did not sell Christ for thirty pieces of silver, kiss Him on the cheek in Gethsemani, then go out and buy a halter. God merely permitted the purchase price of Haceldama to pass from the hands of the high priests to those of Iscariot. You see, then, that this distinction is one that points to a very real difference.

The distinction is introduced here as a preventive. The statement that "Nothing happens but what God wills or permits" is absolutely true. But many people hearing or reading it, neither read nor hear it aright. They fail to see that what God permits He really does not will — else there would be no place for that conjunction "or." One Jesuit theologian put it well when he said: "The will which is called 'permissive,' by which God allows sin and the miseries consequent on sin to be, is undeservedly (*immerito*) named a will; for God does not will those evils, He simply *tolerates* them" (Schouppe, Vol. I, p. 293). So we are not to blame God for the hideous actions of perverse men. But the point we make here is that God can use what He merely permits — and use it for our greater good. He can, and He does, use actual evils to bring about more Christness in this world — and within our own souls.

That being the case, you can understand Paul's wonderful line: "Now we know that God causes all things to work together for the good of those who love him . . ." (Rom. 8:28). We can take that "all things" literally.

You can also understand St. Augustine's line about "God would not permit evil unless He could draw good from it." But never forget it is only a permission, and not a real will. Much more will have to be said on this later. Right now we want some assurance that there is meaning in much that seems meaningless, and something divine in all that seems spewed from hell.

In Paris, where the magnificent Dome des Invalides rises three hundred feet above a sarcophagus of rich red Finland granite, an encircling gallery holds twelve mammoth marble figures in white, each commemorative of some Napoleonic victory. Cut deep in bronze at the entrance to the crypt is the sentence: "I desire that my ashes repose on the banks of the Seine, in the midst of the French people whom I have loved so well." Napoleon's wish was executed magnificently. Emperor Nicolas of Russia gave the elegant sarcophagus, while Prince de Joinville, son of King Louis Phillipe, brought back "the little Corporal's" ashes from far-off St. Helena.

It is an awe-inspiring monument to France's first emperor. But many Frenchmen regard him as the curse of France.

Napoleon has so caught the imagination of men that an estimate of him as the "curse of France" might seem startling. But when one thinks back on his career, sees the fields not only of France but of practically every country of Europe strewn with the bodies of young Frenchmen, thinks on the countless broken homes and broken hearts this adventurer caused, then tries to follow the fortunes of France after this man's fall at Waterloo, the "curse" becomes understandable. Yet Leon Bloy, as passionate a Frenchman as ever lived, could look on this same sarcophagus, conjure up the same magnetic leader, calculate the destruction he wrought, then sum him up as "the face of God in the dark." That is what this deeply religious, if not truly mystic, man saw. Were Bloy living today, unquestionably, what he said about Napoleon he would repeat about Hitler, Stalin, Tito, Khrushchev, and any other of those murdering monsters who have made existence a nightmare and our civilization barbaric. A man like Bloy makes us examine our beliefs and re-examine our thoughts and thinking. God can be in the dark as well as in the light. If He really be God He must be in everything both dark and light, but most especially in those things the legal profession wisely term "acts of God."

Yet Bloy was not original in seeing "the face of God in the dark." Centuries before him, Augustine said the same thing with even greater force about one who was no mere adventuring soldier but sovereign of the then known world. Augustine, in that monumental work of his *De Civitate Dei,* shows how the face of God can be discovered in the features of one as mad as Nero, even as he unleashed that passionately fierce persecution of the Christians. The saint based his reasoning on Revelation. The passage has particular pertinence to our day, and the quote from Scripture may well silence our complainings. Augustine wrote:

> . . . it is in such hands that the Providence of the sovereign God places the exercise of supreme power when it judges that men deserve to have such masters. The divine word is very clear on this subject, for it is Wisdom itself which has said: "It is by me that kings rule, and that tyrants dominate the earth" (Prov. 8:15). And in another place of Holy Scripture it is said: "It is God who rules by knavish princes because of the perversity of the peoples" (*City of God,* I, Chap. 25. Sheed translation).

Augustine lived in times very like our own; hence, he had to meet objections against God such as we hear from every side today. At the end of the fourth century a civilization was crumbling, the Roman Empire was falling apart. Humiliated and angered by the barbarian invasions, the ruling classes turned on Christianity and blamed it for the evils they were suffering. Even in those far-off days it was equivalently said that "religion is the opiate of the people." So you see that there is really nothing new under the sun. But too many of us forget that God has to be over and above, in and around, and under every sun. St. Augustine saw Him clearly in the tyrants of his day.

But the great Augustine himself was not original. This truth is found again and again in Sacred Scripture, especially when things looked as black as they do to some eyes today. God can be seen in the dark. It is enlightening and encouraging to go back to days darker than our own and find them flooded by the effulgence of Him who dwells in Light Inaccessible. We, the Chosen People of God of this twentieth century after Christ, are wise when we study the history of the Chosen People of God in the centuries before Christ and learn, not how wayward humans can be, but how determined God is to have a people He can call His own, how mercy-filled His justices are, how radiant with love is the face that looks at us even in the dark.

You remember how God chose His people. You know something of the patriarchs. But perhaps you know most about the Exodus from Egypt, the wandering in the desert, the arrival in the Promised Land. God had to put up with a lot from them during those forty years: ingratitude, resistance, recklessness, rebellion. Yet there was a brilliant cloud by day and a pillar of fire by night. It was God – lighting their darkness. He finally brought them to the Promised Land; for He is faithful to His promises no matter how unfaithful certain humans may be. You may know little of the subsequent history of this people until the time of David, but surely you know something about him. He slew a giant, became a favorite of a king, and ultimately ascended the throne. In this former shepherd boy God found a "man after His own heart."

Once this intrepid warrior had established his kingdom, it seemed as if God's design was about to be fulfilled: a strong people, vigorously united, totally consecrated to God, would serve Him faithfully and bring to perfection His plan. Humanly speaking we would expect God to use this people as His instrument, have them subdue all other nations, and thus secure God's dominion over all men. But the actual story is far different. After the death of Solomon, David's kingdom was divided. After the division came decadence. Year after year these chosen people of God became more and more like the pagans around them.

God warned His people (as clearly as we have been warned, if not more clearly). They did not listen. Then God took as His allies, as it were, those rulers and those peoples who up to then, and even after, were His enemies. These He used as His instruments. The Chaldeans and the Assyrians, just as the Egyptians before them (and the Communists of today), all unwittingly co-operated with God. They actually collaborated with Divinity, as they executed in time one of His eternal decrees. They helped Him run His world and fill out His plan for mankind.

This is not reading into history. It is but accepting Revelation. Through the lips of Jeremias God spoke and said: "I bring evil from the North and great destruction . . . to make the land desolate" (Jer. 4:6, 7). Lest that be too vague He spoke again through the lips of Isaias: "The Lord will bring upon them the waters of the river, strong and many, the King of the Assyrians and all his glory" (Isa. 8:7).

But that is hardly the first chapter of the story. God has introduced the characters, but He has not made known their real roles. Later on, using the same Isaias as spokesman, He does bare the heart of the matter when He has His prophet say: "I make happiness, and I create misery; it is I who do all this . . . it is I who have aroused Cyrus . . . he will rebuild my city and set my exiles free" (Isa. 45:2–13).

The dark is always lighted by God's face, and He is always looking on His people with merciful love. If we but stare until we see, we will discern in the hard, hate-filled features of today's tyrants what Bloy saw in Napoleon's, what Augustine saw in Nero's, and what Isaias and the people of God could have seen in Cyrus' — the love-filled face of God — our Father.

The trouble is we take only a hurried glance and hardly catch more than the surface sheen of things. We must be adult enough to realize that earth is not our playground, but our battleground. We are old enough and mature enough to realize that only frightened children people the dark with bogeymen; integral Christians find in it the "light of God's countenance" and walk ahead fearlessly as "children of light."

Paul could have been talking to us when he exhorted his Ephesians with the words:

"Awake, sleeper,
And rise from the dead,
And Christ will give you light. . . . Do not act as fools, but as sensible men, putting every opportunity to good use in evil times like these. This is why you should not be thoughtless, but consider what is the will of the Lord" (Eph. 5:14–17).

Reading the Old Testament with an adult mind, that is, staring at events until we see them, one cannot miss the fact that it is God who runs this world — and nobody else. Here and there individuals will act as if they were "Gawd Almighty," but ultimately they will be seen to be little more than puppets who answer to the pull of the strings in the hands of Almighty God. From Genesis to the Apocalypse one fact is luminously clear, and that is that God is the Lord of history. That is why we, in the frights of the present, should realize that God is still leading His people. Today's tyrants have God-given roles. Cyrus of old is among us — and working hard for God, even while he denies that God exists.

But do not fail to make that distinction between willing and permitting!

If you have ever visited a broadcasting station and been introduced to all the departments and men who contribute to the perfection of the performance, or have seen how a television show is put on, you can understand the distinction you must always use between volition and permission. For you have come to know something of the prime importance of the man in the "mixing room" of your radio broadcasting system. He is the man at the controls, and upon his touch depends, in last analysis, what you hear and even the way you hear it. For by the tiniest twist of his dials, he can cause the soft velvety voice of a tenor to sound strident; and make the smoothest of symphonies come to you as sheer cacophony. He controls the broadcast. He does not actually *cause* what you hear. No. The sounds originate either in the throat of the singer or the orchestral instruments. But that you hear them as you do is ultimately and utterly dependent on his *will.*

What is said of the man in the mixing room of a broadcasting station can be said about the man behind the camera in a television production. The way he uses lights and shadows, and the angle at which he pitches his lens is the ultimate reason you see what you do. He does not produce the action. That is done by the actors and actresses themselves. But that you see them and their actions as you do is dependent on the camera man's will.

God is the One behind the camera in the TV show of the universe. God is the One in the mixing room of the world's broadcasting station. That you hear and see what you do depends on God's Will. He does not produce the sounds nor the sights. Men do that. But that those sounds and sights come to you as they do is due to the Will of God. For just as the man in the mixing room by a twist of his wrist can cut off the entire program, and the man behind the camera can black out the whole show, so, too, God.

Why is the cold war going on? Why have some nations been given a blood bath, and some races almost purged from the face of the earth? Why is there world-wide fear of fall-out from atomic explosions, and almost angry watchfulness of the stock-piling of terrible bombs, even as there is sleepless vigilance over the progress of each nation in the perfection of intercontinental missiles, and the tense race for supremacy in the conquest of outer space? Why is it that newspaper headlines so often are nothing but a screech of sin? Why is there so much barbarism in this day of almost miraculous scientific progress?

The perverse will of man is an explanation — and a correct one. But that you personally should be affected by all this, that you individually should see what you see, hear what you hear, and know what you do, is not that ultimately due to the Will of the One in the mixing room and the One behind the camera — God? Is it not true that by an act of His Will not only this man or that movement, but all men and all movement would cease? Is it not absolutely inescapable that all that is now going on is due to His volition or permission?

Grasp that and hold it to your heart: nothing, absolutely nothing, happens in this universe of ours, but by the Will of God or by His permission.

That can well be called the fundamental principle for any man's peace of soul, tranquillity of mind, and calm happiness of heart.

For we know that God is good. In all truth He alone is good. Hence, there must be an ultimate purpose, an infinitely wise and good purpose, for whatever He sees fit to will or permit.

That last gives you what may well be called the second fundamental principle for your joy of spirit — without which no man can really face life today. God has a purpose for everything and for everyone. Paul let us in on an eternal secret. He showed us the Mind and Will of God when he told us that everything and everyone in creation, that all time, from its first moment of inception until that last which will usher in our timeless eternity, points, and ever will point, to Jesus Christ. For if creation was for and through Christ Jesus, much more so is re-creation; for the fact is that creation had to be re-created, our universe had to be re-established; and God decreed "to re-establish all things in Christ" (Eph. 1:9).

This is the fact that brings the living God and His ever watchful providence closer to each of us individually than breath to our lungs. For Jesus Christ makes each individual human being literally of limitless worth. Take yourself for instance. God thought you in His Word before time was. He goes on thinking you now in that same Word. He sees you in that Word. He wills all things for you in relation to, and in orientation toward, His Word — His only Son in whom all are to be "re-established." Why should you ever think of yourself other than as God does? Why should you not see all things as willed by God in your regard to help you become what you are — Christ? Again it is Paul who tells you: "God, who is rich in mercy, was moved with the intense love with which he loved us . . . and he made us to live with *the life of Christ*" (Eph. 2:10). That is the revelation which enables you to understand that other revelation which says: "If, then, any man is in Christ, he is a new creation" (2 Cor. 5:17).

To have been created by God is something stupendous. To have sprung from nothingness in answer to the creative *Fiat* of Omnipotence; to take on being; to possess life; to find yourself possessed of intelligence and free will; to know yourself the image of your Maker and the crown of His visible creation, is enough to fill you with awe. But now to realize that you have been made a "new creature" — and made such by being elevated almost infinitely higher than you were elevated when you came from nothingness into being; for you have been filled with the life that is Christ Jesus — and He is "true God of true God"; to realize this, is to understand what Paul meant when he said: "what really counts is . . . being a new creature" (Gal. 6:15). To realize that divine providence is the Mind of God and the Will of God engaged from moment to moment in your regard, ordering all things for your benefit, arranging every happening in the universe so that you may come to your true human fulfillment — maturity in Christ and as Christ — changes your awe into adoration, and simplifies your life and living; for you know now who you are, what you are to become, and how you are to accomplish it. The Will of God spells life and proper living.

Once a man has grasped this truth he can face up to life with joy, can go forward with fearlessness to the one task which is every man's life task: that of co-operating with God to achieve the marvel He had in His Mind and Heart when He had St. John write: "Behold I make all things new" (Apoc. 21:5). You were made a "new creature" to help God with His "new creation." And everything that God, in His all-wise providence, allows to happen has been planned from all eternity to help you in that work of collaboration with God in "re-establishing all things in Christ" (Eph. 1:9).

In that sense you can see that no matter what transpires, with the single exception of sin, it is meant for your greatest good! You can welcome every *now,* no matter what it holds, as a fresh manifestation of God's love for you personally. You stand, and live, and have your being within that one Reality who is God. His love for you is not only creative, it is redemptive as well. Which means that, once having called you out of nothingness into being, God will never let you go! If you should fall, He will stoop and lift you up into newer being in His Christ.

Centuries before Christ was born, these truths were told us by God Himself. "Behold," He says, "I myself will seek my sheep, and visit them . . . and deliver them out of all the places where they have been scattered in the cloudy and dark day. . . . I will feed them in the most beautiful pastures. . . . I will feed my sheep: and I will cause them to lie down, saith the Lord God."

That is assurance of providence. But to show how personal it all would be, God goes on to say: "I will seek that which was lost: and that which was driven away, I will bring again: and I will bind up that which was broken, and I will strengthen that which was weak, and that which was fat and strong, I will preserve" (Ezech. 34:10–16).

That God was talking about His Christ in that passage is unquestionable when we listen to that same Christ saying: "I tell you the plain truth . . . he who enters by the door is the shepherd of the sheep. . . . He calls his own sheep individually . . . and the sheep follow him because they know his voice." His hearers "did not grasp the meaning of what he said to them," St. John tells us, so Jesus goes on: "I must be very plain with you: I am the door of the sheep. . . . I am the good shepherd. . . . I know mine. . . . I lay down my life to save the sheep" (Jn. 10:1–15).

To sink your roots in God and seek all your growth in devotedness to His Will and collaboration with His providence, it is well to link this prophecy of Ezechiel and the parable of Christ with a paragraph in Isaias where God says: "My thoughts are not your thoughts, nor your ways my ways. For as the heavens are exalted above the earth, so are my ways exalted above your ways, and my thoughts above your thoughts" (Isa. 55:8, 9).

Now that is the point of the prophecy and the parable – and the whole point for you regarding divine providence: just as a shepherd is almost infinitely above his sheep because of his intelligence and can provide them with what is for their best interests, so God is actually infinitely above us in intelligence and can provide us with what is for our best interests. What trust in God should be ours! What courage in the face of every challenge! What unconcern amid universal upheavals! We are "children of light"; for us there is no dark. We are sons of God; eternity is our native atmosphere. We are members of Jesus Christ; the workings of all time are for us and our collaboration with God in the making of "all things new." Divine providence, then, is God's paternity in action in *our* regard.

You know something of what the utter, unquestioning confidence and the complete and unshakable faith of a child can do to the heart of a real father. We are children of God, the oldest of us. Do we want to do violence to His heart? St. Peter gave the directive:

"Cast all your anxiety on him, because he takes care of you" (1 Pet. 5:7). St. Paul gave the reassurance when he insisted that "all things come to pass for your sake" (2 Cor. 4:15).

Stare into the darkness until you see God's face therein. The battle between Light and darkness is not new. It began at creation when God had to say *Fiat lux;* for the earth was void and darkness was over the deep. Since then Light has been the Shekinah – the sign which told of God's presence. Moses saw it in the burning bush. The Chosen People saw it in the pillar of fire at night, and the luminous cloud during the day. When the covenant was made between God and His people, Sinai itself was in fire. When Solomon's Temple was dedicated, it was the bright cloud which showed that God had taken possession of it. When the prophets foretold the Christ, what did they call Him but Light? Isaias said: "The people that walked in darkness have seen a great light: to them that dwelt in the region of the shadow of death, light is risen" (9:2). Zachary echoed him when speaking at the circumcision of his son, John the Baptist, and told how "the Orient from on high hath visited us: to enlighten them that sit in darkness." The Orient was Christ – the Light of the world. It is His face we are to find in every darkness. With David we are to say: "My heart speaks out to you; my eyes strain after you; your Face, O Lord, I long to see" (Ps. 26:8); "O God, restore us: to save us, show your kindly face" (Ps. 79:4). He will. Never doubt it. You will see it if you realize that divine providence is not only taken up with the universe as a whole, but with each of its parts; not engaged on mankind as a totality alone, but on men as individuals. The subelectron in the atom demands Omnipotence, Omniscience, Omnipresence every bit as much as the universe. And the power, the wisdom, and the goodness of God are as interested in and engaged about you, as they were about the Son of the Virgin who was conceived at Nazareth, born in Bethlehem, crucified on Calvary, but who rose from Arimathea's tomb. He has to be, if He is God and Father; for you are His son – and you are to carry on the Incarnation so that there will be a recreation – a "re-establishing of all things in Christ."

CHAPTER FIVE

GOD IS DEPENDING ON YOU... RIGHT NOW

On the first Ember day of spring, mindful of the continual battle between light and darkness, the Catholic Church turns to God as she prays over her people at the end of Mass and cries: "With the Light which is Thy Brilliance, O Lord, clarify our minds that we may be able to see what we ought to do, and having seen, have the strength to do it." This consciousness of struggle is so deep and keen in the Church that the catechumens in the early days were called *photizomenoi* – "those who are coming into the Light." In Christ, the Light of the world, they were going to be made "children of light."

For all such "children," and most pertinently for us, this same day's Gospel has another line which is most significant. Christ had been speaking to the crowds and meeting some sharp objections from Scribes and Pharisees when one in the audience raised his voice in the cry: "Please! Your mother and your brothers are waiting outside, wishing to speak to you." Jesus' reply crystallizes all we have been seeing about God and ourselves. "With a wave of his hand toward his disciples, he said: 'Look! Here are my mother and my brothers. Yes, anyone who does the will of my Father in heaven, is brother, or sister, or mother to me" (Mt. 12:41–50).

If you have never tried to sum up the character of Christ, you have neglected one of the most fundamental duties of your life; for you were made to "put on Christ" as St. Paul said to his Romans (13:14). That is a metaphor taken from the stage. "To put on" there means to assume the character – and act it out. How can you assume the character of Christ and play it out all your days unless you know what that character is? But life is not play-acting. We do more than assume the character of Christ; we become assimilated to Him! Hence, the more pressing necessity for a keen consciousness of who we are and how we are to act. We are *to be* Christ. Consequently, we must know His character most intimately. We can be grateful that He Himself has given us the key to His character — and that on more than one occasion. The words and phrases have varied, but the sketch they drew always reveals the same central structure. If we were forced to sum it up concisely it would be: "Humility expressed in obedience" or "He was faultlessly faithful to His Father's Will."

Such a character sketch is Christ's own painting. Recall the day He sat weary by Jacob's well. The disciples had gone off to town to buy Him some food. When they returned they were doubly surprised: first, to find Him talking with a lone Samaritan woman; and, second, to learn that, after she had gone, He would not eat. They pleaded with Him. "I have a food to eat of which you are ignorant," He said. They did not understand Him; so He clarified His statement and characterized Himself saying: "To do the will of him whose ambassador I am, and to complete the work he has assigned — that is my food" (Jn. 4:34).

Food gives life. If you and I would live as Christ, we must "do the will of him whose ambassadors we are, and complete the work he has assigned us." That accommodation of Scripture is but an elucidation of the work you undertook when you became a "child of light" at baptism. That day you were implicitly put under contract to live as Christ lived, and to be able to say: "I act in no wise at my own discretion, but speak only as the Father has taught me. He whose ambassador I am is with me. He has not left me alone, because at all times I do what is pleasing to him" (Jn. 8:28–29). For at baptism we equivalently said what Paul has Christ saying at His entrance into this world: "Here I am; I am come to do your will, O God" (Hebr. 10:7). If our lives are to be the successes God wishes them to be, we must be able in our last hour to say what Christ said in His. As He stood on the brink of His Passion and prayed His high priestly prayer, Peter and the rest in the Cenacle heard Him say to the Father: "I have glorified you on earth by completing the work you gave me to do" (Jn. 17:4).

The work we have to do is as definitely marked out for us as it was for Christ. It is the Will of the Father. For Him that spelled redemption. For us it spells salvation. We are to continue Christ's Incarnation. We are to complete, as far as in us lies, God's re-creation.

Too often we think of Christ as having come for us men. He did! We sing that boldly in our every *Credo.* But we must never forget that the prime purpose of the Incarnation was reparation. He came to save and sanctify man, it is true; but even more He came to glorify God. He became Man for God before He became Man for men. We have His own word for it in the passage just quoted: "I have glorified you on earth," He says while addressing the Father directly; then He tells us how that was accomplished: "by completing the work you gave me to do" (Jn. 17:4).

In this high priestly prayer, which is called by many "Christ's last will and testament," we find many references to us of the twentieth century and even something of an outline of our life task in the ever present yet always passing *now.* First He presented a petition to the Father on our behalf which, if granted, will enable us to accomplish that task which was assigned us from all eternity but is revealed to us only bit by bit in every new *now.* After praying for the disciples He lifted His face higher and said: "However, I do not pray for them alone; I also pray for those who through their preaching will believe in me." Then came that astounding plea for us of the Age of the Atom. "All are to be one; just as you, Father, are in me and I am in you, so they, too, are to be one in us." Oneness with the Triune God is to be ours. Christ goes on and turns the petition into something of a command: "The glory you have bestowed on me I have bestowed on them, that they may be one as we are one, I in them and you in me. Thus their oneness will be perfected" (Jn. 17:20–23).

You look at yourself and exclaim: "I, one with *God!*" You look about you at the teeming crowds of your fellow men and you ask again: "These — one with *God?*"

A mirror for yourself, and a clear-eyed look at others bring this question to so sharp a focus that you are ready to say that Christ must have been speaking allegory, or that this is an interpolation. But, no! This is revelation. This is the deepest, most important reality in all the world. We are "one with God" – Christ prayed for it. The Father answered that prayer through the sacraments. We are bound to God by His own paternal love. That is the binding force; that is the vital principle of this union. Christ Himself revealed this to us in that same prayer. For He concluded by saying: "Just Father . . . I have made known to them your name, and will continue to make it known. May the love with which you love me dwell in them as I dwell in them myself" (Jn. 17:25, 26).

Those last words throw light on the allegory Christ used to open this final discourse: "I am the vine, you are the branches. One bears abundant fruit only when he and I are mutually united. . . . This is what glorifies my Father – your bearing abundant fruit . . ." (Jn. 15:5–8). Then speaking literally Jesus said: "Just as the Father loves me, so I love you. Be sure to hold my love. If you treasure my commandments you will hold my love, just as I treasure my Father's commandments and thus secure his love. I have told you this, that my joy may be yours, and your joy may be perfect" (Jn. 15:9–11).

The thought gets deeper and deeper, and the reality becomes clearer and clearer as the directive on how we are to achieve success is made more definite. Divine providence is the Will of God; the Will of God is the love of God; the love of God is the life of God; and we live by His life "in Christ Jesus." Therefore, the work Christ had to do is our work; the share He had in the execution of God's eternal plan in time past is our share now. We continue that Incarnation whose primary purpose was to glorify God. We do that by doing His Will from moment to moment, from now to now.

We are engaged in no mere child's play so long as we are on earth, and we move in a fool's paradise – or a fool's inferno – so long as we do not realize that we are *God's coadjutors in the completion of His Creation*. We are on earth to do as Christ did – help the Father "make all things new." To enable us to do that, God had to endow us with a share in His own causality. This He does, not because He is in any way impotent, but precisely because He is omnipotent, and consequently can, and does, delegate authority. Every human being has been given some share in that authority of God; has been commissioned to carry out some part of God's eternal plan; has been given part in divine providence. In that sense Almighty God is depending on each of us right now.

God is God, and the entire universe rests in the hollow of His hand. But to rule that universe He uses the angels and the hands of men — your hands and mine!

For the greatest event in creation He used Gabriel, an archangel. God did not announce the Incarnation Himself. He entrusted the execution of that cardinal point in His entire scheme to another. That was not the first time angels were seen executing divine providence. When Paradise was closed on the first human sinners, cherubim were set before the gates with flaming swords. In the history of the Chosen People you find angels on almost every page and with every personage. Angels were with Abraham, Isaac, and Jacob; angels with Moses and those wandering in the desert; angels with the Prophets; angels in the times of the Judges and the Kings. They came not always as helpers or bearers of good news, as Lot learned when he saw Sodom destroyed, and as Egypt discovered when it awoke and found its first-born slain. Angels are being used today to co-operate with God in His re-creation. You have one; so have I. But the point we make here is that you and I have been made to help God in that same work. He, the First Cause, has shared His causality with every son of Adam and every daughter of Eve.

The truth is being belabored; for it is the only truth that puts dignity into the most menial of tasks. It awakes us to reality, and sharpens our consciousness to the fact that to be "natural" we have to be supernatural; for the economy in which we live is God's economy; and, thanks to His prodigal paternity, that economy is supernatural. All of which means that if we would be ourselves, we must be Christlike. There is only one Way to live — just as there is only one Truth and one Life — He, *Christ.* And that is the simplification of what so many moderns have complicated. The beauty of it lies in the fact that to reach the maturity that counts with God we have to become like little children. It was Christ

Himself who taught this truth — and taught it by illustration. Ear was not enough for this fundamental verity; eye had to play its part too. So "He called a little child to him, and placed him in front of them [His own disciples]. 'I tell you frankly,' he said, 'if you do not change and become like little children, you will not enter the kingdom of heaven. Therefore, he who, like this little child . . ." (Mt. 18:3).

Modern man does not like the idea of becoming "like this little child" simply because he does not know what Christ meant. It is St. Paul with his lines about "When I was a little child, I spoke as a little child, I thought as a little child. Now that I am grown to manhood, I have discarded as useless my childish ways" (1 Cor. 13:11), who appeals to the man of the twentieth century. But let us note well that Paul spoke of "child*ish* ways," while Christ spoke of becoming child*like*. One commentator on this passage proffered the explanation that when Christ said "like this little child" He pointed to Himself. That explanation is unique among the commentaries on Scripture. But when we stare at the character of Christ as we have just seen it, and compare it with that description of the child given in the past chapter, we see that this exegesis is uniquely apt. Christ had that "utter, unquestioning confidence" in His Father we spoke of; He manifested that "all-expecting dependence"; but above all He, like every good child, was perfectly obedient to His Father. He always did His Father's Will!

Once modern man grasps the meaning of Christ's charge to "change and become like little children"; once he learns that Jesus inculcated anything but the sentimental, soft, weak, babyish nonsense that is sometimes presented as Christian maturity; once he learns that it is not the sweet, moving, defenselessness of the child that Christ wants, but his simplicity, his sincerity, his genuineness, his acceptance of reality, and his energetic entering into it without calculating the gain for himself, modern man will be avid to acquire it. It is the child's absence of what we call shrewdness, cleverness, sly selfishness that is the childlikeness Christ would have His disciples — both those of long ago and those of today — cultivate. It is no easy achievement; for, as Christ said, we have to "change." We are overmature in many ways and about many things, even while being most immature about the things that really matter.

The childhood we are to cultivate springs from faith and the fact that God is our Father. Once we have that truth working in the very marrow of our bones, then we are not only ready, but anxious to accept everything as it comes from our Father's hands — no matter what the nature of the thing proffered, nor what the consequences of our acceptance. We are on tiptoe to take it; for we know our Father is all-good, all-wise, and all-powerful. The true child of God sees the hand and the heart of His Father in everything and everyone who in any way touches his life. That is why he is always calm, always confident, always warm with deep, permeating joy. But to arrive at this attitude of mind and cast of soul, we ordinary men must live by faith — and that requires effort — great effort in the beginning — of mind, heart, and will. But once that effort is continued and the attitude achieved, then you have that faith which "overcomes the world." You have attained to real "victory" (1 Jn. 5:4). To become a child in Christ's sense is to arrive at genuine Christian adulthood, and to be alive with earnestness for one accomplishment: the Will of God. It is to have found out what life is all about — and to be somewhat surprised by its simplicity. "Thy Will be done!" sums it up.

You have said this prayer, which Christ taught us, from the time you could lisp. Who could count the number of times you have said: "Thy Will be done"? But have you even once realized all that is contained in that phrase? Full cognizance of what is meant by it will lead you into reaching the final fathom in the truth about divine providence. It means that God is caring for you every split second of your existence, and that His care is that of a loving Father, and that just as truly as God cares for us every moment of our existence, so we should be caring for God every moment He allows us to live on earth. When we plead that His Will "be done on earth as it is in heaven," we are implying that His Will — the Will of the only Omnipotent — can be frustrated. That is an alarming, an appalling statement. Yet it is absolutely true; for it is Revelation.

In teaching us how to pray, the Only-Begotten of the Father revealed to us the weakness, as it were, of Almighty God, showed us the quasi-dependence of the Infinitely Independent, and manifested to us a certain impotence in the only Omnipotent Being. We are not playing with words. This truth was given us by God's only Word – Jesus Christ. It was He who told us that the all-holy Will of God is entrusted to the weak, wavering, sinful, selfish wills of men. Because God made us free, we can frustrate His whole plan. We have already done it. Paradise was lost to man by man.

"Thy Will be done on earth as it is in Heaven. . . ." What are we praying for? His Will are the decrees and determinations of His providence – all that He foresaw and decided should be. Therefore, God's Will is what ought to take place here on earth among men, just as it is what actually does take place in heaven among the saints. In heaven His Will is done – what ought to take place, takes place. But here on earth, men are of such minds and wills that we must pray to God continually, begging Him to see to it that His Will is done here below. But the amazing part of this prayer is that we can answer it! For if His Will is to be done on earth, we are the ones to *do* it; and we are to do it freely. God, having endowed us with liberty, will never take it back. He wants His Will to be done on earth by men who enjoy and who employ the utmost freedom.

". . . as it is done in Heaven." Have you ever stared at the material heavens above you until you saw how God's Will is done there? The sun, moon, and stars are God's creatures. They play a part in His providence. They contribute to the carrying out of His eternal plan in every new *now*. How faithful they are! So faithful are these creatures to God's law that we human beings can tell time by each of them. This obedience to the specific law of their being glorifies God, executes His providence, fulfills His Will. What a lesson for man!

"Thy Will be done on earth . . ." Yes, we have some pedagogues closer to hand and just as capable as the sun, moon, and stars. We have the mountains and the plains, the rivers and the seas; we have the earth, winds, rains, seasons. From any, as from all, we can learn the secret of successful living. They all obey Him. The winds and the waves on Gennesaret's Sea obeyed the Son of God. The winds and the waves on all the seas of the two hemispheres obey God the Father. Time and tide, although they wait for no man, do wait on God.

What is true of inanimate nature is equally true in the animal and plant kingdoms. Plant an acorn and you'll get an oak. Sow wheat in the fall, you will get material for your bread in the early summer. Where would we humans be if these creatures of God were not obedient to His Will in their regard – if H_2O made water one day and carbolic acid the next; if a rosebush bore loveliness one year and the poison of hellebore or hemlock the next; if a pair of Maltese cats gave a litter of furry beauty from one mating and nothing but cobras and copperheads from the next? Fidelity to God's law spells life for them – and life for us! How truly it can be said that God depends on them for the execution of His plan and the realization of His providence. Nature is faithful. What of supernature? Does freedom have to spell infidelity?

Inanimate nature will follow nature's law without human enforcement being necessary. But what of that law which is natural to man, and is God's Will in his regard?

Every kingdom we know is ruled by law. On law is founded all our sciences. Chemistry, physics, biology, geology, astronomy, and all the rest exist and advance only because of the stability of what we call the natural law. But God is the God of nature as well as of supernature. So that natural law is God's law. Being His law, it is His Mind and His Will; it is His love. That law is written into the beings of everything from a glow worm to the burning sun, from a particle of dust to a flaming seraph; and man is no exception. God's law is written into our beings. But since we are moral beings, it is called the moral law. Yet it is still God's law, God's Mind and Will, God's love. And just as the acorn will reach maturity as an oak only by following God's law and abiding in God's love for it, so man will become what he is only by fulfilling the moral law; for that is God's Will in his regard. There, then, is where we will find that peace for which we burn; there is the secret of successful living.

Obedience to this law gives us our greatest liberty even as it leads us on to our one worthwhile accomplishment — Christhood! We do well to call it natural law. We do better to call it moral law. We do best of all when we recognize it as God's Will for us — His love for each of us individually. For it is only by following this law, by fulfilling this part of God's eternal plan, that we can become what we are; for we are truly human only when we are partly divine. The economy we live in is supernatural. God is depending on us to further His design. We will do it if we behave like "children of light" and obey our law.

Without us God's providence will bog down. He depends on us for the perfecting of His eternal plan. But for that He does not ask us to be as steadfast as the stars, immovable as the mountains, regular as the seas, unchangeable as the sun. God asks us only one thing: to become what we are — moral beings. That is His Will for us ordinary men.

But we must realize that there is a challenge to our morality, to our humanity, in the deepest sense of that word, in everything we touch.

We can limit God's Will for us men to the moral law, and identify that with the Decalogue Moses received on Sinai, only if we understand just how far that Decalogue goes. Its ramifications are found all over our human world: our personal lives, our social, domestic, political, civic, economic, and our national and international lives are all governed by this one moral law. Morals maketh man, and every aspect of our human living has a moral connotation of one kind or another which stems from one of the Ten Commandments. That is the way God writes law — it is of universal import and utterly timeless in its essence, though it may vary in its application.

That is why, to the man who asks us *where* he will find God's Will in his regard, we can reply: "Everywhere." And to the one who should ask *who* will reveal God's Will to him, we can say: "Everyone." And to those who inquire in *what* is a man to find God's Will, we say: "In everything." Should anyone ever ask *when* shall God make known His Will to us, we can say most emphatically: "Right *now!*"

The piercing point of this truth is not only that we can and should find God's Will everywhere, in everyone and everything, all the time, but that we ourselves, with all our liabilities and frightening limitations, are part and parcel of divine providence, and must manifest God's Will to others by our lives.

We ordinary men lead such lives of routine and seeming meaninglessness, that we shun with something like terror any close scrutiny of what we are doing with our years. We awake today and hurry to work as we did yesterday and the day before. Tomorrow it will be the same story. Our work never changes essentially. We are always at the same machine, desk, or chair; always using the same instruments or tools. After a morning of labor, we dash to lunch. Then back to the same routine until the whistle blows or the bell rings. Then we hurry home to an evening meal, read the paper, watch a TV program . . . "and so to bed." Tomorrow will be no different. Where in this is the thrill? inspiration? dignity?

There never will be any unless we stare at this overfamiliar routine, and keep on staring until it begins to look most strange; until this drumming monotony suddenly discloses the face of God. Your job and mine are elements in divine providence. Your job and mine, the things we work at now, were seen by God before the world was, and decreed by Him to be our jobs today. Therefore, as we go about what seems so humdrum, we should wake up to the fact that right now God's eternal plan depends on what we are doing. That gives eternal meaning to our every gesture and divine significance to each fleeting moment. Your work and mine are God's Will for His world through us! Do you see, then, that we are, as it were, the extremities of His fingers, through which He is giving a touch of perfection, maybe a touch of beauty, to His world *now?*

We have to open our eyes to see reality. We have to stare before we can recognize God. We look at some group huddled in a ghetto, and see nothing but pitiable foreigners. We gaze at a swarm in some slum, and see nothing but indigence, incompetence, filth. We watch some subway entrance belch forth its human lava, or some factory pour out its "hands," and we think we are really seeing them when we shudder at the thought that these are eternal beings, made to the image and likeness of God.

But that shudder shows how little we know of God, of man, of ourselves, and divine providence. If we would only stare until we really see, we would recognize the splendor and magnificence of our all-beautiful God; we would see in them His wisdom, His power, and His goodness. For we would realize that they walk only because the Eternal and Immutable walks in them. If they work, it is only because Omnipotence depends upon them. They are extensions of that all-wise hand which "reaches from end to end mightily and orders all things sweetly" (Wisd. 8:1).

How easy it is to see the face of God when we search for it! It is in the lineaments of those princes and prelates of the Church who rule our various provinces, in those of the bishops who reign over our dioceses, of the pastors and priests who run our parishes. His all-holy face can be seen in those tens of thousands of teachers, religious and lay, male and female, who strive to give youth a foretaste of heaven by imparting to them some knowledge of "the one true God and of Him whom He has sent — Jesus Christ."

Yet it is not only in these and such as these that God's face is easily discernible, but it is clearly recognizable in anyone who has any authority. There are many ways of looking upon our president and his cabinet; upon the Senate and the House; upon the governor of our state, the mayor of our city, and the selectmen. But the clearest view of them is had when we come to recognize them as co-operators with God in the execution of His providence. Christ's words to Pilate are key words. When he told the Roman governor that he would have had no power over Him whatsoever had it not been given him from above, Jesus was not referring to Rome so much as to His Father in heaven. Paul's words — "there exists no authority not ordained by God. And that which exists has been constituted by God" (Rom. 13:1) — are familiar enough, but do we ever apply them to — say — the policeman who commands us to stop? If we look aright we will see in these often weather-beaten countenances the face of God. These men are co-operating with Divinity. They are carrying out God's providence.

God is depending on these men for the furtherance of His creation. They are helping Him complete His eternal plan. And if they realized what they were doing, would they themselves not look upon their work quite differently?

But it is not only those in authority who help God; it is all of us. The farmer, as he plows, plants, cultivates, is working with God, forming a partnership which is to produce the harvest. Just as he depends on God for proper weather, so does God depend upon him for the intelligent and freely given care of seed and soil. Providence is a partnership. The miner burrowing into the bowels of the earth should feel the very breath of God on his neck; for he is doing in time what God had decreed to be done from all eternity. The same is true of any and all workers. The factory "hand" at his position in the assembly line, doing nothing all day long but inserting bolts or tightening nuts, is as much a part of God's providence as is the president or the pope. Actually – as with all on earth – he is either improving God's world or marring the perfection of God's plan. Let him do his task well, and he has done the Will of God; He has answered his own petition of the *Pater Noster:* "Thy Will be done on earth . . ."

Man must awake to the fact that God is in the ordinary every bit as much as in the extraordinary. No one questions divine providence being behind the Deluge or the destruction of Sodom and Gomorrah. Everyone will admit God foresaw and ordained that Jerusalem should be flattened, that He decreed the eruption of Vesuvius and at least allowed that earthquake which reduced San Francisco to rubble. There is no difficulty in seeing this. So with other history-making happenings. We all realize that it was part of His providence that Columbus should seek India and find America; that Marconi should stumble upon the wonders that have given us wireless, radio, and television; that Einstein should conceive the formula which would enable us to split the atom. But we should realize also that God foresaw and ordained such ordinary things as that you should be reading this book. Such seemingly insignificant things as the elbow work of the bootblack, the button-pushing of the elevator boy, the gearshifting of the cab driver, the dishwashing of the housewife contribute to that "making all things new" which is the ultimate in God's providence. Paul said "all creation groans and travails in pain until now" (Rom. 8:22). Have you ever once realized that it was groaning and travailing because of you? Paul also says: "All creation awaits with eager longing the manifestation of the sons of God" (Rom. 8:19). So you see that it is not only God who depends upon you right now, but all creation! For what Paul says here, Peter says with more concreteness: "We look," he says "for new heavens and a new earth, in which holiness dwells" (2 Pet. 3:13). This first Pope tells you that you are not only to await, but that you are to "hasten the coming of God's day" (3:12). You do that by doing God's Will *now*. For the delay is due, commentators tell us, to the fact that we have not repented in the basic sense of that word; we have not changed our minds and hearts; we have not "become like little children."

So you see that the more Christian we become, the more clearly we realize how precarious a thing is this precious Will of our Father. It is the most powerful thing in existence – for it is God; yet, it is ever in jeopardy because entrusted to what has proved so often the weakest thing in creation – the free will of man. That is why we must beg God to see that His Will is done – and ask for strength that we may be faithful to that partnership which is divine providence, and do that Will of His in our own particular sphere. The more profoundly we penetrate into our personalities, the more powerful becomes the conviction that the one absorbing passion of our lives should be the Will of God; for then the purer becomes the concept that our Father, who is in heaven, is depending upon us, His sons on earth, right now.

Too long have we been satisfied with what the biologists and philosophers have given us as the definition or description of life for man. They say it is "the union of soul and body," for they clearly see that what we call death ensues when body and soul are separated. But that is as truncated a definition of human life as is the definition of human origin which says that "creation is the production of something from nothing." Both are omitting the most essential element. Creation is the production of something from nothing *by the action of God*. It is untrue to say that "man came from nothingness." He came from God! So with human life: it is the union of body and soul *with God.* For He alone is Life — and the sole Source of all that lives. *To live is to partake of God!*

David has a psalm contrasting the living God with the lifeless gods:

> The heathen idols are but silver and gold,
> the work of human hands.
> They have a mouth, but do not speak;
> and they have eyes, but do not see;
> and they have ears, but do not hear;
> and in their mouths there is no breath.
> Like them are all that fashion them,
> and everyone that trusts in them (Ps. 134:15–18).*

There can be no partnership with such gods; no union that would be fruitful. But with the living God union spells deathlessness. Christ said that He was the Life; that He came that we might have life "and have it in abundance" (Jn. 10:10); that He was the Bread of Life, "the living bread" which "if one eats . . . he will live forever" (Jn. 6:51); that "no one that lives and believes in him shall be dead forever" (Jn. 11:26). Joined as we are to the living God, we are eternal beings; and are true to ourselves only when we live and labor to complete God's eternal plan — which is dependent on the *now.*

---

* Kleist-Lynam translation.

CHAPTER SIX

LET YOUR LIGHT SHINE... NOW

...AS YOU WORK

The going has been hard. We have been asked to believe that we "have all the time in the world." We soon found we couldn't deny it – though it still has a disturbingly peculiar ring to it. We saw that time is continual motion which comes from Him who never moves. That took a little thinking but we finally saw it could not be doubted, let alone denied. But then we were startled by the truth that what we call divine providence entails not only God's care of man but man's care, as it were, of God. Yes, the going has been hard. The last stretch was about the hardest; for we learned that the prayer we lift to God, asking that His Will be done, is one we must answer ourselves; for His Will depends on ours for its fulfillment. We cannot question these facts. Nor would we ever experience any difficulty in accepting them had we really believed what we so glibly profess to believe; namely, that we are made to the image and likeness of God! Face the fact: we don't believe. We shrink back from accepting the tribute God Almighty pays us. We don't believe He grants us a share in the running of the world. We don't believe divine providence is a partnership. Small wonder that we are lost.

Let no ordinary man bridle at the charge. The evidence is overwhelming. If we believed what we profess to believe we would be sanctifying the world in which we move. But what is the fact? The world transforms us instead of our transforming the world. We are drifters. We never take definite direction. Caught in the swift, and ever swiftening, current of our times, we are swept along with the crowd and find ourselves thinking thoughts that are anything but Christian, let alone Catholic; accepting principles that will never square with the Gospel; indulging in practices that have been condemned by all the modern popes; surrendering our selfhood to the serfdom of present-day economics; looking upon work as something imposed by an unkind fate and something we will be wise to get rid of as soon as we can and in any manner possible. Labor we think demeaning, yet dare to call ourselves followers of Him who was called "The Village Carpenter." Christ was a worker — because such was the Will of the Father for Him. Christians must be the same — and for the same reason. That shows what a privilege it is for man to labor; for it is a condescension on the part of God to take man into partnership with Himself.

This truth must penetrate until it becomes so much a part of us that we live and move in an almost constant awareness of God and His immediate presence. We ordinary men need an inner rule, some bedrock, immovable principle to act as our compass needle, or we will always drift and ever be lost. If we are seriously seeking the Will of God, we cannot fail to find that rule and principle; for it is He of whom all Scripture speaks. Thomas Aquinas put it in a sentence we would do well to memorize and actualize. Thomas said: *"Totum principium vitae nostrae et operationis nostrae, est Christus"* (*Comm. ad Philip,* c. I). Which means that the one, ultimate, total principle of our lives and actions is *Jesus Christ.*

In the fullest sense of the word, a Christian is one who belongs wholly to Christ. Therefore, for all who call themselves Christian, life can be simplified, dignified, integrated, and divinized by a total commitment to this principle who is a Person. Such a commitment is true wisdom! For, without a vision, men die. They may go on existing, but they do not live. With Christ as our vision, all that is good, all that is great, kindles within us, and we flame with a faith in our own greatness — that surprising and surpassing greatness which is a gift from God — that share in His divine providence.

The workers of the world have been called to look upon more than one vision this past half century. The most common and captivating is that of a classless society in a world that is one. But that is not a vision. That is a mirage. Yet millions are following it as do thirst-mad wanderers in a desert—to their own destruction. The vision God gives to the workers of the world is not one that has to do with any impossible future, nor one that has to do with the past alone. It is one that catches up past, present, and future in the *now*. For the vision held out to us is that of the Eternal Son of God, whose hands once became hard and calloused from work, and who is still our contemporary. Jesus Christ, who ever did the Will of God, is our Vision. And, in all truth, without this Vision *men die!*

This truth must permeate our whole beings if we are to really live. Plato, a pagan, reached these deep, dark fathoms when he taught that "the wise man is he who imitates, knows, and loves God, and finds his happiness in participating in God's life." That happens to be not only a perfect description of a Christian but a perfect summation of the purpose of this book. It also shows you the value of the Vision now being presented to the workers of the world. Jesus Christ, the Galilean Woodworker, has given us a knowledge of God that leads to love, a love of God that spurs to imitation, and an imitation that sets us craving—and getting—more and more grace, which, as St. Peter tells us, is "a participation in the very life of God."

It is not only honesty, it is prudence, that will now have us confess that we have not only been shortsighted but totally blind. We have not seen our way through the world simply because we have not seen ourselves for what we are according to God's Will, and what the world is in that same divine plan. But now we have a Vision. He is the Light of the world. He can cure us of that blindness and, open our eyes to reality, to the splendor of God's world and the magnificence that lies in man's work in that world. Let it be repeated that it is not only sight we need, it is Vision; it is Christ, who is Splendor; Christ, whose face is aglow with God's glory.

There is no doubt about it: we are at one of history's turning points. A world-wide and an almost unfathomably deep revolution is in progress. Because of recent discoveries in science, economics, and politics, changes have taken place which entail a recasting of our social structures. Our entire universe seems in some sort of ferment. But that does not call for any jeremiad. Granted that we have witnessed profound upheavals in almost every sphere of human endeavor these past few decades, what follows? Even granting that the disturbances have been more universal and much better known than any that took place in the past, that is no grounds for fear or crippling anxieties.

Moralists who are blackly pessimistic about the future are forgetting much of the past. Our present-day evils are not intrinsically different from those of yesteryear or earlier times. We are simply seeing and hearing more about them. Since Adam listened to Eve there have been evils in the world. Yet, amid them, history — God's story — unfolded. Call it God's story, for He is the Lord of history. The events we chronicle are but the unfolding of His eternal plan. So, relax! Everything *is* under control!

Philosophers predict disaster. In recent revolutionary developments they see such a complete departure from the past, such an utter rupture of relation with traditional European culture, that they can foresee nothing but a universal relapse into barbarism. They paint a picture of our age as one not only disillusioned about the past, but despairing of the future. But such philosophers are not philosophizing; they are merely lamenting. A real philosopher always goes on to ultimate causes. Today's genuine philosopher will find the Ultimate Cause of our universal upheavals to be the Prime Cause of the universe. So again we say: Relax! Everything is under control — God's! For when we trace things back to their Source, we always look into the eyes of God, find the hand of God holding things firmly, and come to know the Will of God for us now.

The truth of the matter is that every age has had its upheavals — and men have bewailed them. Six centuries before Christ, Jeremias sang his lamentations about the evils of his day. And there were those who grew fearful and foresaw naught but disaster for their civilization. Yet those dark days were followed by "the glory that was Greece and the grandeur that was Rome." Five centuries after Christ, Salvian pointed to the evils of his day and promised succeeding generations little but woe. Yet his particular darkness was followed by the dawn of the Middle Ages whose heyday was "the thirteenth, the greatest of centuries." Today there is no need to lament, but great need to be alert to the opportunity God is presenting us at this period of His providence. Every great historical rebirth has been issued in by a long night of struggle, and finally emerged only after torturing trials. Before us today are two utterly irreconcilable ideals; two pitched camps in neither of which can any compromise be admitted. But the directive is still: "Relax! Everything is still under control!" The real upheaval and the true conflict lie in those two camps and in those two ideals. But that is nothing new. It is as old as what happened in heaven when Lucifer refused to serve; as old as what happened in Eden when Adam failed to obey. It is as old as creation itself. That is why we can relax; for the conflict is all part of God's providence. It falls under His permissive Will.

But because it is only His permissive Will that allows it, we can never be passive in the face of it. Relaxed we will be; that is, without any foolish fears, any semblance of panic, any sort of insane anxiety. But at the same time we will be alert and active, keenly and sanely anxious to do the Will of God *now* . . . even "as it is done in heaven!"

Right now we are watching the last convulsions of a dying world. Capitalism, as we came to know it – *laissez-faire* capitalism – is dead. We need not lament its passing; for it had deteriorated from the original aims and ideals of an acceptable system, and had lost its primitive spirit entirely. History tells that at its inception capitalism was spurred on by a grand spirit of conquest and animated by a lofty spirit of service. In those days it did wonders for humanity. But, once it was established, the spirit vanished, and even the spur of conquest became vicious. Then some capitalists became utterly selfish and unbelievably inhuman. The code of those capitalists was anything but Christian. It was greedy, grasping, totally lacking in any *mystique,* essentially materialistic, and of this earth most earthy, as it centered and even concentered on self. There was absolutely nothing heroic about it, nothing really manly, since it was without any mystical element or real significance. Thank God that is dead and buried. But, of course, that death and burial did not change God's original plan about private property, private enterprise, or personal labor. That passing did not so much as bring an illness to individual initiative and proper class consciousness. That is why we can speak of today's capitalism as the capitalism of the people.

The collapse of the old capitalism brought with it the collapse of that stratum of society which had been its base. We are now watching the emergence of a new society. For that, too, we can thank God; for change is a sign of growth, activity is proof of vitality. It is the emergence of that new society that gives us our greatest opportunity. We "children of light" must make this world brilliant. We members of Christ must see to it that this new society is shot through and through with substantial spirituality. Now is the time for us to teach the worker members of this society how to relate time to eternity, work to worship, and labor to love of God. That is His Will for us *now*.

Obviously God's Will is that the late twentieth century should see a new civilization. Our century has been savage. Its first five decades brought horrors that make the bravest of us blanch. And in the present the antics of governments have sane men wondering if they will stupidly plunge ahead and shake the very pillars of the universe with the goods God has allowed them to discover. To the most superficial student of history it is evident that the past five centuries have been naught but progressive departure from God. The emphasis was placed on the things of this world and the heaviest accent was set on man. We have called it humanism. But that is a misnomer; for we have already seen that the only acceptable description of a human must bring in God. Yet the name is with us, so we must qualify it as a mean and pitiable humanism; for it not only would do away with God, it did away with the best in humanity — thought! Compare those mighty works of real human thought found in Aquinas and Dante with anything the past five centuries produced, and you will immediately see why we have called it a "mean and a pitiable humanism." But it turned out to be also an utterly inhuman humanism as it went from the gradual minimization of the importance of God to Nietzsche's cry that "God is dead," then on to the cry of the militant atheists that there is no God and religion is but an opiate. This mean humanism progressed steadily until it reached its nadir in concentration camps, furnaces such as Moloch never knew, extermination of races, and the veritable jungle which is called our political world.

But even this gruesomeness and Godlessness was all under God's providence. His respect for human liberty is like Himself – it is infinite. Yet, God can always bring good from man's worst evils. He permitted the smart men of the past five centuries to go their way; He has allowed some of the very clever men of our own century to go theirs. But with what result? That humankind would be saying "There is no God"? Just the opposite! With reason one wonders if ever in all mankind's long and varied history there was a time when men were seeking God with such seriousness as they are right now. The lesson learned from the past five centuries is that humanism is not only unsatisfying; it is a total failure. The outlook is so bad that men are forced to look up. Men *are* seeking God today though they may not admit it. But the fact is that the present ruin of the world is the Christian's greatest opportunity.

Christianity itself has been purged in the process, and already a "new Christianity" is being born. Accidentally new, of course; for the essentials never change. But how marked are those accidentals: Liturgical Movement; lay apostolate; native clergy, here, there, and everywhere; the prestige of the Papacy; the deepening of knowledge about God and self; and the lively interest in the profoundest spirituality. But the one thing needed perhaps most of all is the Christianization of work and workers.

Do you ask why? The answer can be: Because such is the Will of God right now. To the most careless observer it must be evident that the class liberated by the death of *laissez-faire* capitalism is to be the class which will exert the greatest influence on the civilization that is emerging. The workers of the world are the dynamic element in this new civilization – and they must be "baptized" if there is to be justice, charity, truth, peace, and happiness upon earth. The fate of the immediate future, which unquestionably will spell the fate of the world, lies with Catholic and Christian workers. If they "baptize" their work and their world, mankind is saved. And they are the only ones who can do it. For, unknown to itself, the world of workers is seeking the Gospel of Jesus Christ. He, "the Way, the Truth, the Life," gives the only ideology that will help solve mankind's problems and simplify all its perplexities. But He can present it now only through His members! That is why

Catholic and Christian workers of the world can say that "their hour has struck."

Analysts tell us that the youth of today, who are the real workers of the world today and tomorrow, are not as interested in inert money as were their elders. What they crave are creative opportunities, and the employment of their energies in labors that will change the world. They want intense life — and they are determined to live intensely. Finally, they have a sense of solidarity never known before. If this analysis is correct, then truly this is "the hour" for Catholic and Christian workers of the world. For where or when was there a more total demand made on anyone than that made — and renewed every day — by Christ? His disciples must be ready to leave all. They may not turn back for so filial a task as the burial of a parent. Where will youth find a solidarity equal to that of the Mystical Body or the Communion of Saints? Where is greater activity demanded or the fullest employment of energies required than in campaigning for Christ and so changing the world as to make it the Kingdom of God?

But this "baptism" cannot be one of water. It must be one of "blood." It will take red-blooded men with wills as strong as steel. For this generation exemplifies Edgar Guest's observation perfectly: They would rather *see* a sermon than *hear* one. Men today are intensely concerned with earthly interests, and the principles of Christ are primarily spiritual. Yet that does not mean that the present generation will not accept those principles. It only means that we Catholics and Christians must incarnate them in our own flesh and blood. Humanity listens to spiritual messages only when those who bear them live them. Was it not Pascal who said: "I believe witnesses who get their throats cut"? Which, after all, is but another description of Christ and real Christianity. So the Catholic and Christian workers of the world must show their co-laborers a Christianity that is utterly faithful to its original inspiration; completely devoted to Christ; and totally without compromise of any Christian principle. Our contemporaries are exacting in their demands for sincerity in any who would offer them a doctrine for life and proper living. We have the truth about labor — and even about labor organizations. We have the truth about social justice and genuine charity. We have the truth about God and man, about God's Will for man. Now is the time for us to live those truths—especially when at work or among workers.

This "baptizing" begins with ourselves. We must come to a vital conviction that Job was right when he said: "Man is born to labor as birds to fly" (Job 5:7). Hence it is God's Will that we be workers. It is according to His plan and His providence that we labor. God Himself worked at creation. His only Son, who became one of us, labored. So, far from degrading man, work gives him a dignity that is somewhat divine; for it enables him to share with God the labor of completing the world.

Incarnate Wisdom told us we cannot serve two masters. Do we really believe Him? The passage in which that line occurs merits incorporation here. It is excellently well put in the Kleist-Lilly translation:

> The fact is, in dealing with their own kind, the children of the world are shrewder than the children of light. And so I say to you: money is a worthless thing; but use it to make friends for yourselves, so that, when it gives out, they may receive you in the everlasting homes. He who is conscientious in small things is conscientious in big things also; he who is unscrupulous in small things is unscrupulous in big things also. Therefore, if you do not prove conscientious in handling so worthless a thing as money, who will trust you with a genuine good? And if you do not prove conscientious in handling what is not your own, who will trust you with what is your own? A servant cannot be the slave of two masters; for either he will hate the one and love the other, or, at least, be attentive to the one and neglectful of the other. You cannot have God and money for masters (Lk. 16:9–14).

Is it not too true that most of us serve Money six days a week and give the seventh to God? It is a fact that the Decalogue demands that we keep holy the Sabbath. But, by that specification, the Decalogue does not give us leave to desecrate the other six days of the week. Speaking with the authority of God, the Church gives us a precept about assisting at Mass on Sunday. But, by so doing, she does not free us from the obligation of worshiping God every other day in the week. For, just as we are not Americans and patriots only on July 4, April 19, May 30, and November 11, but Americans and patriots every day in the year – every year. So, too, we are children of God, creatures who owe Him worshipful obedience every split second we breathe.

But more than half our waking hours are devoted to work. What correlation exists between your work and your worship of God? Do you go to your place of employment with the same attitude of mind and orientation of souls as you do when you head toward church on Sunday? Or have you permitted divorce between your religious life and your economic living – with separate maintenance for both? Many have! But without realizing that, if they do not find God in their work, over half their lives are spent without conscious communing with the only One through whom they can live. God did not half make us. We are not part-creatures. We owe God worship with our whole beings every hour we live. But if there is no direct relation between God's Will and our work, between our lives of labor and our loving God, how can we keep the First Commandment of the Decalogue, let alone the Third?

There is so much confusion in modern man's mind concerning work, the best plan of attack is to go back to the original idea God had in His Mind when He made man. He made us to His image and likeness. That means we are the image and likeness of the Creator who worked six days, then knew a Sabbath's rest. God Himself explained the Third Commandment for us when He gave Moses the Decalogue saying: "Six days shalt thou labor, and shalt do all thy works. But on the seventh day is the sabbath of the Lord thy God" (Exod. 20:9, 10). Then, as if to connect up the idea of our image and likeness to Himself, God went on with: "in six days the Lord made the heaven and the earth, and the sea, and all things that are in them, and rested on the seventh day: therefore, the Lord blessed the seventh day and sanctified it" (Exod. 20:11). It is God Himself, then, who has ordained that we spend six sevenths of our week at work. Yet it is the same God who has commanded that we love and adore Him with all that we have and all that we are. So there simply must be an interrelation between work and worship; for both are the Will of the one true God for each of His human creatures.

But this Will of God about work is not only in the Decalogue.

Genesis gives it as clearly, if not as explicitly, as Exodus. For, even before he had tasted the forbidden fruit, Adam was a worker. "The Lord God took man, and put him in the paradise of pleasure to dress it, and to keep it" (Gen. 2:15). So it was not sin that brought work into the world. Had Adam not taken the fruit we would still be workers; for work is a share in God's labor of love, which is creation. Sin did bring a change in the plan of God about work; but it is not an essential one. It brought in sweat, strain, weariness. But it did not deprive the worker of the pleasure God wanted him to have in a job well done; nor did it change the role of man in God's creation. Even after being banished from Paradise, Adam was still the crown of God's visible creation, still shared in God's own Lordship of the world, and was still God's chosen agent to carry on creation. We, children of Adam, fell heirs to that lordship – to which work is our title. Once we lay aside the title, we cease to be men as God meant men to be.

It is, and has ever been, God's Will that we work. Christ's pontiffs, again and again, have pointed to the dignity of the laborer, and fearlessly scolded those who would "outrage that human dignity which God Himself treats with reverence" (Leo XIII, *Rerum Novarum*). But the point being stressed here is the dignity, the sublime and surpassing dignity, of labor itself – it makes one kin to God. It is a point that has to be sharpened for our wrong-thinking man of the mid-twentieth century. For, despite the lesson history so imperiously teaches, namely, that when manual labor is looked down upon, civilizations crumble, we, of this crumbling civilization, still look down upon manual labor. Greece is before us. So is Rome. So, too, the late Middle Ages. Yet we will go on aspiring to the white-collared class, envy the so-called gentleman of leisure, and blush over our "servile" employments. And all this two thousand years after the hands of the Christ of God had been calloused from using a plane and a saw; two thousand years after God's only Son sweated at a carpenter's bench and became weary from hard, manual labor. What manner of men are we? What kind of Christians?

Although we know it is God's Will that we work, and have Christ's example that it be as humble, docile, cheerful laborers, yet here we are within a split second of God's eternal judgment seat and we relegate our worship to the Sabbath and God to the sanctuary. Then we wonder why our age needs so many tranquilizers, is so tense, anxious, and filled with fears. Work is God's specially appointed tranquilizer, stabilizer, and means to adulthood. God planned labor as a way for us to express our inner wholeness and a means to manifest our lordship over inanimate creation.

Atheistic Communism has already unwittingly done some wonderful work for God. It will yet do more. The pressure of its propaganda and its facility in coining catch phrases have been such that we have been alerted to the hollowness behind many of our own catch phrases and the deceit in much of our own propaganda. We went along for decades without ever challenging *laissez-faire* liberalism in economics or politics. The same is not true today. Phrases about "natural liberty" – "equal rights" – "free competition" – "individual initiative" – "rugged individualism" – and "survival of the fittest" are met with demands for definitions and clear explanations. For we know now that so-called liberalism leads to selfishness and greed. What was accepted once as "rugged individualism" is recognized now as sheer avarice – which St. Paul, under divine inspiration, named "the root of all evil." Too well do we know that what went under the title of "free competition" or "free enterprise" went on to produce economic slavery and the death of individual enterprise. So we are seeking solid principles and asking for contact with honest reality and real honesty. Both the quest and the questioning are ended for those who have found their God and know His Will about work. But the actualization of that honesty and the presentation of that reality have hardly begun. That is why we can now thank Marx, Engels, Lenin, and even Stalin. . . . But, no! We can only thank God for having used them and their darknesses to open our eyes to light – the Light of the world, that only Son who was a worker of Galilee. We can thank Him, too, for granting us this unique opportunity for the "re-establishing of the workers' world in Christ Jesus." But gratitude, like love, is shown more in deeds than in words. We must "let our Light shine before men. . . ."

But have we got the Light? That is one of the most serious questions any ordinary man will ever be called upon to answer honestly! You have seen burnt-out electric light bulbs. Seen from the outside they often seem to be intact. But they cannot give any light, for the filament within is dead. How are we to light the world of workers if the filament within us is not alive; and how can that filament be alive unless made deathless by the only truly Immortal One; and how can that deathlessness be maintained without constant contact with the Christ of God? The question is again posed: Have we got the Light? We are not going to Christianize labor and the entire world of workers unless we ourselves are truly Christian; but we cannot be truly Christian unless the Light of the world burns within us; but the Light of the world cannot burn within us unless we let Him.

God's gifts have often caused God to grieve. You can see this in the first book of the Bible where you read: "It repented him that he had made man on earth. And being touched inwardly with sorrow of heart, he said: I will destroy man whom I have created . . ." (Gen. 6:6, 7). You can see the same thing in the first book in the New Testament. Jesus says: "Jerusalem, Jerusalem! Murderess of Prophets! Stoner of the messengers sent to you! How often have I been willing to gather your children as a mother bird gathers her brood under her wings! But you refused it!" (Mt. 23:37.) God grieves because men do not accept His gifts – or, accepting them, do not use them aright. Now is the time for us to awake to the fact that baptism gave us a filament that need never burn out; but it is a filament that will never light up unless we allow the current who is Christ to flow through it. In other words since life is action, Christian life must be the action of Christ in us and *through* us. Christ will never shine out on our world unless we allow Him to burn within us. We can be the same as "burnt-out bulbs" even after baptism; for many of God's gifts are but potencies that must be reduced to act – they are filaments that must be set aglow, and it is man who turns the switch, as it were, to let the current through. Grace does not work automatically; it requires man's co-operation. We must *live* our religion and not simply profess it with our lips. We must radiate Christ. But that is an impossibility unless we are aglow with Christ, unless our convictions are flaming convictions.

How do you look at your boss? – there is a test as to your possession or nonpossession of the Light within you. If your attitude is one of subservience, you are dark. If you have only respect, you are not really light. If you have only anger or envy, of course you are really black of heart and soul. Your boss may be a blackguard. He may be as unprincipled as the Politburo, a scoundrel of the first water, a public sinner. Yet, if his authority is legitimate, you will not only respect him, you will show him reverence. Not for what he is, but for what he has; "for he is God's minister for your benefit" (Rom. 13:4). If he has authority, it is from God; for Paul was absolute in his inspired statement: "there exists no authority not ordained by God" (Rom. 13:1). He drives it home by obverse iteration: "that which exists has been constituted by God." With that truth aflame within you, your attitude toward all those in authority will radiate the attitude Christ had before Pilate, before Caiphas, before His very executioners. It will be reverent. It will not be subservient! Have we the Light?

If we really believe what we so glibly profess to believe, then we know that every detail in the milieu in which we now work has not only been foreseen by God Almighty, but willed by Him. The ones under whom, alongside of whom, or over whom we work have been chosen, as it were, hand-picked by God as our co-workers for right now. That does not mean that we are to stay with the same group or hold the identical position we are in at the moment for our entire lives, but it does mean that we can worship God, radiate Christ, and grow toward genuine maturity by seeing them all as part of God's eternal plan — and manifesting our gratitude toward them for their obedience to our Father. The word "charity" is very like the word "liberty." It is granted plenty of surface for existence, but is allowed next to no depth for resonance or reality. Charity is not veneered politeness. It is not suavity, urbanity, good manners, or good breeding. It has an inner depth these will never know. Charity is of God; and it is warm with God's own warmth. It can be felt from those who have the Light. It will be felt by all our fellow workers if we are aflame with Faith's own convictions about labor and our co-laborers; and it will be felt under no other circumstance. We cannot give what we do not have. Have we the Light?

Dr. Alexis Carrel has claimed that the fundamental cause of our decadence is a loss of "a sense of holiness." This deeply thinking man is not talking about any vague religiosity, any kind of cosmic pantheism, and certainly not any sort of compromise between poetry and science. He is talking about precisely what we have been thinking about right along; for a "sense of holiness" comes down to an awareness of the presence of God! Not the god of the scholars or the philosophers, but the one true living God, the God of the people, the God who rules all, and whose Will is made clear in every event of history, in every happening in time. This "sense of holiness" comes from the Light within. If we have it, we will go to work — no matter what the nature of that work — with the same attitude of soul and purpose of will with which we go to church. For it is as much the Will of God that we work all week, as it is that we worship on Sunday; and cheerful, grateful obedience to that Will is Christian life and living. It is the highest tribute we can pay God; for it is using our highest faculty — our will — as He wills us to. It is, therefore, truest adoration. We worship as we work, or we do not work aright.

CHAPTER SEVEN

REALIZE... RIGHT NOW ...THAT YOU HAVE A GOD-GIVEN CAREER

Rudolph Allers summed up our situation once by saying: "At bottom, there is only one ideal — 'doing one's job in life' — involving self-surrender and service; in the same way there is really only one virtue — humble, *volitional conformity to the will of God* — and only one sin — defiance of God's will. . . ."*

No theologian will object to that statement. No philosopher can question it. No psychologist will not applaud it. But you note how simple he has made life, and the formation of real character; for that is precisely what he was treating at the time. He ended by saying "Catholic life, based on Catholic principles, can reconcile the antitheses of our being and bring about a resolution of tension." In our language that means peace and happiness.

Thomas Verner Moore, another psychologist and psychiatrist, has put the same thing in a slightly different manner:

> To the religious-minded man God is the Supreme Intelligence in a universe of intelligent beings. And as the Supreme Intelligence in this universe of intelligent beings, He is directing all minds to an end conceived by Himself and worthy of His own transcendent powers. . . . And so we may say that the Supreme Intelligence exerts His omnipotent power to bring to its realization an end that in its fullness only Infinite Intelligence can conceive, but in *which finite intelligent beings can participate.*

* *Psychology of Character* (New York: Sheed & Ward, 1943), emphasis added.

That fairly well sums up what we have been saying about providence being a partnership. But then he goes on to speak of work:

> One who has really made a religious philosophy of life the great living force in his mental activity can view his own humble lot with patience and contentment. He realizes that in order to live and accomplish something worth while he need not attain to any position of great political importance, nor become a man of great wealth and influence, or even be blessed with good health and freedom from trial and sorrow. But it is necessary to submit his mind to the guidance of the Supreme Intelligence and devote his energy day by day to accomplishing in the most perfect manner possible the duties that each day imposes.*

We have not taken in the entire day. We have reduced our concern to the only time we have, the only time there is, the only time there ever will be: the *now*.

Dom Moore went on to show that ordinary men who have a real philosophy of life — and there is only One — *Christ*! — can endure

> with patient self-denial the hardships, disappointments and monotony that one must suffer to the end that *a life's work may be finished*, and an unselfish contribution made to the welfare of humanity and to that eternal order which the Supreme Intelligence is establishing in a world of intelligent beings.

The vocabulary is different from our own, but the truths are the same: providence is a partnership. Let any man do his duty — no matter how humble — and he has contributed something to the fulfilling of God's all-wise plan of "re-establishing all things in Christ."

> There is much more poetry and idealism in the lives of plain, ordinary people [says Dom Moore] than the pessimism of some can possibly imagine. . . . The privileged few in our days sometimes think that they alone can relish the higher things in life; but in factories and offices, in tenements and hovels, thousands know and appreciate truths of which the (so-called) better classes have no understanding. . . .
>
> And so it is with the honest everyday life of the honest everyday man. The idealism is there. He does not see it himself, but when

---

* *Personal and Mental Hygiene* (New York: Grune and Stratton, 1945), p. 81. By permission.

> he has lived out his life faithful to the end, a poem has been written, a work of religious value has been accomplished, and a contribution made to the divine order that God is bringing out of the chaos of human sorrows and perplexities, wanderings and doubts, labors and strivings that seem, but only seem, to end in failure.
>
> Religion alone can enable the toiling thousands to understand the meaning and value of life's monotonous drudgery and so to endure sorrows that would otherwise be unendurable and to carry burdens that would otherwise be insupportable.*

The only point on which we differ from the eminent psychologist and psychiatrist is that we do not find any "monotonous drudgery" to life. We find labor – plenty of it. But with St. Augustine we say: "Where there is love, there is no labor. Or if there is labor, it is loved." In other words we love the Will of our Father. Since His Will is that we labor, we love labor; or better, we labor for Him whom we love.

Such a concept of reality, and very especially the reality of work, does not keep us from sweating as we labor, or from growing weary from our work. But it does put us very much in the attitude of mind of Him who sat weary by Jacob's Well and then refused the food the disciples brought Him saying: "I have a food to eat of which you are ignorant. . . . To do the will of him whose ambassador I am, that is my food!" God's Will is food, drink, and life – to those who are wise.

It is the Will of God that each of our lives be filled to the overflowing with meaning; that each of us be an important individual; that we each know a real career while on earth, and leave it only after an accomplishment which will have eternal repercussions.

That reads like nonsense to the materialists of our day. But, then, what was ever more nonsensical than materialism or a materialist? The paragraph reads like nonsense to those present-day realists who insist on seeing things in the raw and calling them for what they are. But, then, such realists never come into real contact with Reality! They see only the surface; and, in this case more than in others, "appearances are most deceiving!" We have already seen what lies below the savage surface of things and people – *Christ!*

---

* *Ibid.*

That paragraph remains. Each statement stands. For if each human being who breathes in this present now has not a special career to fulfill for God, and is not, therefore, truly important to Divinity, inasmuch as he or she has some contribution to make to the execution of that plan drawn up in eternity, then Infinite Wisdom has gone witless, and Infallible Omniscience is stupidly blundering. For if God be God He is breathing in everyone who is *now* drawing breath, and theology tells us that God never does anything bootlessly. Philosophy says, too, that no one ever acts without a purpose. If God be God that purpose can ultimately only be Himself. Hence every living human being has, and is *now* enacting, a veritable career: one that comes from God and is for God. Further, there is no such thing as a negligible human being. And, finally, who can escape the conclusion that there is no such thing as a useless old man or old woman, a useless or underprivileged child, a useless and even burdensome new-born defective? Since God is God His every creation is good, and His every human creature has an exalted career!

That is not put down to build up the human ego but to show that the only thing that really matters in this world of men and this era of time is the Will of God.

We need to be staggered by the truth; for we move among men who will worship the mysteries latent in the atom, yet refuse to bow down before the atom's Creator. These men will cry for "plain truth and high living"—but what the world needs is plain living on the heights of such truths as we have been facing. The air is purer on such an elevation, and is better not only for our physical systems but for our immortal souls as well. R. L. Sharpe has put it in verse entitled "A Bag of Tools":

> Isn't it strange
> That princes and kings
> And clowns that caper
> In sawdust rings,
> And common people
> Like you and me
> Are builders for Eternity?*

---

* From *Best Loved Poems of the American People,* edited by Hazel Felleman (New York: Garden City Book Co., 1936), p. 99. By permission.

That sweeper in the subway; that cripple begging at the subway's entrance; that blind man feeling his way down the subway's stairs; that mongoloid child staring so vapidly at the passers-by, its harassed mother tugging its arm; that drifter pulling his frayed coat closer against the wind; that "man about town" meticulously lighting his cigarette – all these building *now* for eternity? Yes, and what is more, each is carrying out a God-given career!

How reconcile such a concept of reality with what a public-relations man for Dun and Bradstreet has written? A. M. Sullivan, calling for men of three dimensions, commented thus on the contemporary scene:

> A nameless horde moves through life in a stupor of selfishness, its vision dulled in mediocrity, its conscience numbed by materialism, its loyalty sworn to the obvious. This human caravan is not composed wholly of clods and zombies. Among them are men and women of education, of social position, of business achievement, of professional excellence who are possessed of a blind ego and obsessed by personal greed. They carp and claw, seeking preferment, advantage, and profit at the expense of others. Lacking the three social dimensions of understanding, generosity, and compassion, they cannot stand on their own feet, but must lean on, or feed on the virtues of a neighbor. They add bulk to humanity, momentum to the flow of mankind toward destiny, giving some power to the wheels of the world's economy in their production and consumption of goods and the creation of physical wealth. But they contribute little to the spiritual resources of the day in which they exist, and bequeath no worthy treasure for posterity's delight.*

This man, who ought to know what he is talking about, has not told the whole truth – even about these people who only exist. For even these have a place in that scheme of things called divine providence, and it is God alone, the real Director of Public Relations, who knows that place, and can see that they fit it to His satisfaction. Even if each in this "horde" should be a "clod" and a "zombi" according to this man's estimate, it would still be true that each is an immortal being, made to the image and likeness of God, and precious enough for a God to become man and die for it. Hence, he or she would merit not only respect but reverence!

* *The Three Dimensional Man* (New York: Kenedy, 1959).

It is clever men like this who need a man like St. Paul to set them rethinking their tough thoughts about other human beings. Paul had to do it to his Romans, his Corinthians, his Ephesians. Need we wonder that we have to echo him to our fellow Americans? "By the commission that has been given me," wrote St. Paul, "I say to each one among you: Let no man esteem himself more than he ought, but let him etseem himself in moderation according to the degree of faith which God has appointed to each one." Paul was addressing the Christians huddled in the Roman ghetto. Monsignor Ronald Knox says this, more than likely, was written from Corinth. The Corinthians had been blessed by God by many and diverse spiritual gifts. But human nature, even after being elevated by grace, being what it is, there were rivalries, jealousies, unhealthy competition, odious comparisons, and disunion. Therefore, Paul thought it wise to warn his Romans against too great a preoccupation with spiritual and special gifts. The big thing was faith. The real gift, incorporation in Christ. So Paul reminded them: ". . . just as in one body we have many organs, yet not all the organs have the same function, so we, the aggregate, are one body in Christ, but individually to one another we stand in the relation of part to part. We have gifts differing according to the grace that has been given us. If the gift is that of God's inspired spokesman, let it be used under the control of faith; if it is ministry, let one minister, or if one is a teacher, let him teach, etc." (Rom. 12:3–7.) Ronald Knox makes the point for us when he comments: "This is an Epistle to remember especially when tempted to draw too sharp a line between the natural and the supernatural. . . . An Epistle to comfort us when we feel — as most of us do these days — that we are only cogs in a machine. Excellent!" exclaims the Monsignor; "for cogs also work for God."

If any generation should realize that there must be cogs, we are of that generation. Can any machine run without them? But how excellent it is to be a cog in God's machine — and to have been fitted by Him into the one place we are needed, and to contribute something to the smooth efficient running of the machine.

This is a truth that must grow in and with us. It is to be a living truth even more than a truth by which we live. For the time has come when technology has not only eliminated most of the strain and sweat from work, but also much of human skill, human ingenuity, and almost the human individual himself. This leveling process is true not only in the field of labor, but also in the other fields of human activity as well. The machine, which is part of God's providence, and a very kind providence at that, is becoming Frankensteinian. Planned by God for the development of man, it is being used by men to destroy the individualism of the human being. Automatic devices do reduce the hours of drudgery, but that reduction has not yet produced what God meant it to: a stairway to the stars for the former drudge. He has become less of a menial, perhaps, but no more of a man; for his importance as an individual has been lessened.

Undoubtedly this is one of the causes of the mental fog in which so many modern men move. Outwardly they do not count. They are made to feel this by the very nature of their employment. Yet inwardly they are conscious of some sense, no matter how dim or vague, of being a superior part of creation. Almost instinctively man knows he has an identity, and suspects quite profoundly that he is an integral part of some sublime superhuman mystery, and he is fascinated by the personal import of this suspicion which gives him a personal importance in the universal scheme of things. There is the tension in modern man. There, also, his sense of frustration. Technology makes him little more than a clod. Theology tells him he is kin to God. The solution lies in the realization that even clods are important to God; that human nonentity is filled with genuine grandeur; that individuals considered unimportant by men have, in the unerring eyes of God, an intrinsic value that is infinitely beyond all human assessment.

No human can be satisfied so long as he thinks his days are but "crackling and going up in smoke." Made to the image and likeness of the Creator, man wants to create! Man must achieve or he walks in a world of gloom no matter how brilliant the sun outside him. If our psychologists wish to find the "primary" that has made this generation the "angry generation" let them look at the book of Genesis and learn the career God has determined for every human being. "And God created man to his own image; to the image of God he created him. Male and female he created them. And God blessed them saying: Increase and multiply, and fill the earth, and subdue it, and rule over the fishes of the sea, and the fowls of the air, and all living creatures that move upon the earth" (Gen. 1:27, 28).

There is the Will of God for man and woman. God never changes. There is the Will of God for present-day man and woman, you and me. We have a God-given career. It is a threefold assignment. We are to image forth God. That is number one – and it is an assignment from which we are never free. Every passing moment of the day and night it is incumbent upon us faithfully to mirror forth our Maker. Volumes have been written on how we are to do it. Volumes yet remain to be written on how we are to do it. Yet it can be summed up in one word; the word St. John the Evangelist used to describe and define God. "God is *love,*" he said. Therefore, if we humans are to be what God made us to be, we must love. Do you ask whom or what we must love? The answer is like our God-given career; it is threefold. We must love God, self, and neighbor. But whoever heard of anyone loving another and having a will different from the beloved's? If we love God we will make our life's ambition, our life's work, our life's dedication that of doing His Will. The second part of our generic career is to fill the earth, to bring forth a posterity for God. This, of course, for most people means marriage. For the few others it means the more difficult and demanding task of bringing forth a spiritual progeny who will praise God. The third part of our career is to become lords of the earth, air, and sea – rulers of the world.

God's plan being such, and man's employment of the machine being what it is, there is no cause for wonder if the "lords of the world" grow angry when reduced to "hands," "numbers," "nonentities." A "creator" must feel like a caged eagle when set standing beside an unconcerned machine day after day with nothing more inspiring than switches and wheels before him. If the eagle beats its wings against the bars of the cage, and screams as it longs to soar toward the sun, no one need wonder if among workingmen resentment becomes righteous indignation and finally boiling anger. Genesis can speak to more than psychologists and psychiatrists; it has much to say to social scientists, management, labor leaders, and all who employ fellow men. God's Will is that each man, in his own way, be a lord of the universe. No one can oppose that Will with utter impunity even in time.

But what we ordinary men need to know is God's Will in our own individual lives. We know we have been called into being by our Creator, and are preserved in that being by the same Creator, that we, with the rest of our fellow men, may mirror God, assist Him in His providence, and thus rule the world. That is our generic career. It is one we share with all men. But even in the following out of that career there is an individuality that none of us can dare miss without ruining our lives. We have been sent into this world by God with a specific role to fulfill. It is our duty and our delight to find out that role. It will be our destiny to fulfill it.

Let us realize that we have been sent from God just as Gabriel was sent from God to Nazareth; as John the Baptist was sent by God first to the desert, then to the Jordan; as was God's only Son sent from the bosom of the Father! Our mission is as real as were those three missions — and wonder of wonder, our mission, like each of those, is intimately connected with and concerned about the Incarnation of God and the Redemption of mankind. That is the Will of God for us ordinary men. That is our career — *to be Christ.* And what He said about His mission, we must say about ours: "It is not my mission to condemn the world; but, on the contrary, to save the world" (Jn. 12:47).

It is fact that we do not feel like saviors of the world; we who have a tiny position anyone else could fill, or a trifling job anyone else could do. We ordinary men often wonder just what life is all about; for everything in our ordinary day seems so insignificant. We make about as much impression on our age as a ship passing through the sea, or a bird flying through the air. Yet here is Sacred Scripture indicating that we are saviors of mankind.

If we go on thinking blunderingly it is only because we have never taken an open-eyed look at Jesus Christ our Savior. He was so ordinary that not only his fellow townsmen in the tiny town of Nazareth, but His own blood relations, those whom the Scriptures refer to as His "brothers," looked upon Him as our contemporaries view us. He was no great account to them. When He began to teach and preach they shrugged their shoulders and asked: "Is not this man the son of the carpenter? — And his mother, is not Mary her name? — And his brothers — are they not James, and Joseph, and Simon and Jude? — And his sisters — are they not our next-door neighbors? How, then, did this man come by all this?" (Mt. 13:55.) In other words the Son of God was looked upon as a nobody and a know-nothing, from nowhere. It is not often that Christ is seen in focus. Look at Him as Man. Remember where He was born, and of whom. In a cattle shed of a peasant girl who had married a small-town carpenter. Remember where He was brought up. In Nazareth, a despised town of a despised province. Remember His nationality and race. He was of a despised people. He was the poorest of the poor. That is how He was born, that is how He lived, that is how He died. He had to use the manger cattle use at His birth. He had to use a criminal's cross for His deathbed. Then He had to be buried in a borrowed grave.

Next, look at the work He did. For eighteen years He worked as apprentice to a carpenter, then when the carpenter died, He inherited his shop and his trade. Nothing great about that, is there? When He went out to teach and preach, how many really understood His preaching or accepted His teaching? He worked miracles — raised the very dead to life. Yet, even this unimpeachable testimony was impeached. He was called Beelzebub's workman. He was said to have a devil. He was named a Samaritan by His own people. Still, this Man who lived so ordinary and insignificant a life for thirty years, then knew such opposition, frustration, and finally complete failure, is the Man who saved the world. He did it by doing what we ordinary men are asked to do now — *God's Will.*

We need to read the Gospels with imaginations that are accurate and eyes that see the reality set before us. Christ, the Man who saved mankind, was ordinary in the eyes and estimate of His contemporaries. Twenty centuries of faith with their wealth of painting, sculpture, and architecture; twenty centuries of faith with their intellectual geniuses among Fathers, Doctors, and ecclesiastical writers; twenty centuries of faith with their magnificent Councils of the Church, so color our picture of Jesus Christ, the Son of the village carpenter, the Child of Mary of Nazareth, that we almost fail to see Jesus Christ at all.

Romano Guardini asks us to suppose that, on the day of Christ's triumphal entry in Jerusalem, "a high-ranking Roman officer in shining armor had trotted by on his blooded mount, his orderly troop behind him, a fragment of that great army which bore the power of Rome across the world. What would this man have thought had he seen a poorly dressed man on a donkey, a coat as a saddle, the heterogeneous crowd around him?" Guardini admits that the thought hurts, but he insists that "that is how it was." So we see that even what we call the triumphal entry was shabby as the world appraises things. Our Christ was not great according to the standards with which we are too familiar. He saved the world by doing the Father's Will — as if to say there is only one greatness for any man. That is the greatness to which we ordinary men have been called. Our career is a Christ-career. We must save mankind by doing as He did.

No one can overstress the fact that Jesus Christ was pleasing God the Father, praising the Godhead, and saving mankind every moment of His earthly existence. Good Friday and Easter Sunday were the climax; they were not the totality of Redemption. Your salvation and mine did not begin when Pilate condemned Christ to the cross, but when the Triune God sent Gabriel to Mary of Nazareth. Calvary and the empty tomb are but the last lines to that life and death which spell eternal life for all who believe and do the Father's Will. To put it pointedly let us say that God the Father was as pleased with God the Son when He took His first baby steps and knew His first human fall as He was with that same Son when He took His first steps toward Golgotha and knew His first fall under the cross; He was getting satisfaction from what the Boy Jesus did at Nazareth to help His foster father in the carpenter shop or His mother around the house, as well as when that same Christ was scourged at a pillar and crowned with thorns; He saw reparation being made for mankind's enormous sins as Jesus sweated in the workshop at Nazareth just as He saw it being made as Jesus sweated blood in Gethsemani. Christ's lifework was the reparation of the Father's glory and the redemption of men. That lifework, that reparation and that redemption, was being effected during the

Flight into Egypt just as well as during the Way of the Cross. To sum it all up in a word, let it be said that *obedience* saved the world—and nothing else did. Nothing else will save it now.

Once the ordinary man realizes what happened to him at baptism, the fright and hopelessness generated by the challenge to be a savior vanishes. We all know that Jesus Christ alone redeemed mankind. We all know He alone could make adequate satisfaction to the Creator of men who had been so outraged by the sins of men. But what we do not seem to appreciate is the fact that we have been selected by God for the wondrous career of continuing and, in our own sphere, completing Christ's work. That is God's Will for each of us right now. That is our real career.

You wonder anxiously: "How can I ever continue Christ's work? How can I help save mankind? I—Why I can't even help myself at times. To save my own soul appears something more than I can do. . . ."

That is precisely the point of calling your attention to baptism. What is utterly impossible to you as a human being has been made comparatively easy for you as a baptized human being. Baptism was a rebirth. You were born again. But this time you were "born of God"—as every priest says at the end of every Mass. When you were first born of human parents you came forth from the womb with a human nature. That nature is the principle of all your human acts and operations. If you had not received from your parents a nature like theirs, you could never function as a human being. But at your second birth you came forth from the "womb of the waters and the Holy Spirit." You were literally "born of God." You were made a new creature. Since you were "born of God" you came forth endowed with a share in God's own nature. Your second birth made you someone almost infinitely more powerful and precious than did your first birth; for your human nature had been elevated almost measureless realms above the merely human. This re-creation of you was something more marvelous than what happened when God first said *Fiat* to nothingness and brought a universe into being. If the Triune God, at the close of each day of creation, could look at the completed work and see "that it was good" and even "very good," what must be said at the close of each day of re-creation when men are baptized in the name of that same Triune God? Words are inadequate; worship is the only proper action. But every ordinary man, so selected by God, should realize that he has been given a new nature in this new birth which makes him a new creature. We have been given a share in God's own nature. It follows then that we can do God's own work. *Agere sequitur esse* – "Actions spring from essence." You can fulfill your Christ-career, for you have been made Christ. That is what christening – or baptism – means. If, thanks to having been made a man, you can do manly things, then, thanks to having been made Christ, you can do Christly things. You can save the world. You can do the Will of the Father *now.*

The fact merits one more attempt at clarification. What is the physical difference between a dead man and one who is fully alive? The dead man has every organ the fully alive one has; but the heart does not beat, the lungs do not breathe, the blood does not circulate. He lacks the principle of vital activity. That body has no soul. It is not endowed with human life. So you, without grace, were as dead as that human corpse as far as divine vital activity was concerned. Your soul lacked a "soul" – a vital principle, a source whence divine activity and divine life could spring. You received it in baptism. Once you have been baptized in the name of the Father, and of the Son, and of the Holy Spirit, you breathed with the very life of God. This is revealed truth. St. Peter, the first Pope, told us that we "become partakers of the divine nature" (2 Pet. 1:4). Peter meant exactly what he said: "we become partakers of the divine nature." That does not mean that we become God Himself; it means that we become His adopted sons, His children, His co-workers, His heirs. What Jesus Christ was by nature, we become by grace. Therefore, our career is the Christ-career; and it is possible of fulfillment in Christ, through Christ, and with Christ. We have all we need in nature and in grace. All that is required for triumphant success is our obedience – our doing the Will of our Father. The Greek Fathers of the Church were realists. They called things by their correct names. That is why you so often read words such as "deified" and "divinized" when you con their writings about baptism and the baptized.

The fact is there: we have been made more than human. Our souls have received something above the human, something above the natural. Thanks to that elevation, we are capable of doing God's Will just as His Only-Begotten did it — and with the same results: glory to God and salvation to men.

Pius XII in his encyclical *Mystici Corporis* struck off the career of Christ and the careers of Christians in a sentence: "When He would redeem mankind, the Word of God willed to make use of our nature; that the work begun might endure He makes use of the Church . . ." that is, of Christians. Having taken a physical body to achieve redemption, He has taken a Mystical Body to accomplish salvation. What He did in and through the members of the Body He took from the womb of Mary, He wants to continue in and through the members of the Body He has taken from the womb of mankind. He wants to obey. He wants to do the Father's Will. But He cannot do in His Mystical Body what He did in His physical Body unless we co-operate with Him. He cannot obey unless we obey. He cannot do the Will of God unless we do it.

With those facts before you, you can understand why Pius XII broke out into the exclamation: "Nothing more glorious, nothing nobler, nothing surely more ennobling can be imagined than to belong to the Holy, Catholic, Apostolic, and Roman Church. For in that Church we become members of one Body. . . ."

There is God's Will for every man. He wills that we become members of His Son's Mystical Body; that, in it, "every man will perform a work of collaborating with Christ in the dispensing of the graces of redemption." God wills that each of us have a share in the salvation of mankind. That is why it can be said with absolute theological truth that God *needs* us. "Not that He is indigent and weak," as Pope Pius XII pointed out, "but rather because He has so willed it. . . . In carrying out the work of Redemption He wishes to be helped by His members. . . . Deep mystery this. . . ." But what could be more stimulating and comforting than to know that God needs you to complete the work of Christ on earth?

By this time you must know that your Christ-career does not call for any miracles on your part. You do not have to cleanse lepers, multiply loaves or fishes, change water into wine, walk on water, calm wind and wave, or raise the dead to life. Your career is not one demanding that you speak as no man has spoken before you. Nor is it one that requires a scourging, crowning, and condemnation to a criminal's cross. None of these things, in themselves, or in the life of Christ, would have saved the world, had not each, at its particular moment, been the Will of the Father for the Son. For once again we insist it was obedience, and obedience alone, that undid Eden's harm. What redeemed mankind then will save men now. But Christ is waiting to use your will in order to "do always the things that please" the Father.

And those things are exactly the same as He did when He appeared as an ordinary Man. That is precisely what the Father wants from Him. Nothing else will please Him. Nothing else is required to save a race. Never forget for an instant that God wants to "re-establish all things in Christ." That is why time goes on. That is why history is being made. And you have a career to work out in passing time — which will be your personal history. That career may be a difficult one as humans estimate things, but it will never be anything but simple so long as you focus on the one thing that matters: the Will of God for you now.

You can learn how simple it all is from the greatest Woman who ever lived. Mary of Nazareth never did anything great in the eyes of her fellow humans, yet there never was, nor will there ever be, a career to compare with hers — save, of course, that of her Son. Mary is Mother of the Mystical Body — and its most exemplary member. What she sang of herself in her *Magnificat* is something every Christian can sing with the same literal truth; for God has "looked as graciously on our lowliness" and we can rightly exclaim: "How sublime is what he has done for me" (Lk. 1:49). But have we done for God anything similar to what Mary did? That is the question of all questions. So let us see what she did. She said *Fiat* — "Be it done to me . . ." or as the Kleist-Lilly translation has it, perhaps somewhat more clearly: "May all that you have said be fulfilled in me!" (Lk. 1:38.) That is the magic word: *Fiat*. It was with that word that God began creation. Here we see the beginning of re-creation, and it is by the same word. If you learn that word and all that it means, then act upon it; your career is an assured success. You will have pleased God as did Mary and Mary's Son. You will have effected, inasmuch as in you lies, the same as they effected by their fully free *Fiat*. Christ used this word, remember, at that other turning point in man's history — when He, the God-Man, writhed in agony in the garden of Gethsemani. But, lest you again fall into that too common error, that this is all beyond you and your powers, look at Mary for a few moments and see what she did to become the Coredemptrix of the world. For that is your career in a single word.

Once again we have to make a profound effort to be realistic and see things as they were — not as two thousand years of love have made them appear. We can hardly think of our Mother without awe. We see her truly "clothed with the sun." Everything about her is splendor. But how did the people of Nazareth see her? Granted, now, that everything about her is steeped in mystery; that she lives and breathes in closest contact with God; that there is majesty and marvel connected with her every action. Nevertheless, when studied objectively, even the second joyful Mystery of Mary's Rosary will show that God's Will is wrapped up in what is ordinary. For what girl, with just ordinary sensibilities, would not have hurried to the aid of an aged cousin who is said to be with child? Now we all know that this Visitation contained within itself mystery piled on mystery: Elizabeth recognizing Mary as Mother of God; John the Baptist, yet unborn, recognizing the incarnate God who had just been conceived; Zachary cured of his dumbness; and all three living principals prophesying. Yet, the Visitation itself — that "setting out in haste to go into the mountainous region," to help her kinswoman — was a very matter-of-fact deed. No real girl would have hesitated a second before doing as Mary did.

The same can be said — with like qualifications — about the other Joyful Mysteries. Not only ordinary girls, but every ordinary man, is to "bring forth Jesus." We are all to "mother the Christ." That is why we were born — and reborn. The Presentation was an act common to every Jewish woman who brought forth a child. So it would have passed unnoticed had not Simeon and Anna been inspired by God. So, as far as Mary and Joseph were concerned, it was a very ordinary action.

As for the final mystery in the Joyful five, what mother and father would not have done precisely what Mary and Joseph did? Who would not "retrace their steps to Jerusalem, there to renew their search for him"? And once they had found their child, what mother would not cry out in the very words Mary used? So you see how very matter of fact these very mysteries are. When viewed with the eyes of contemporaries, they are seen to be most "ordinary." Yet, it was these ordinary actions that saved mankind and allowed Mary to live out her career as Coredemptrix.

There is no need to "go down with them and come to Nazareth" in order to see how ordinary was the life of the world's Coredemptrix; for we have already glimpsed the fact when we saw how Jesus' own relative looked upon Him when He began to preach.

Outwardly, everything in the life of Mary was quite ordinary. She did the normal things any other girl or woman placed in her position would have done. Yet it was by doing them that she helped Christ satisfy God and save men. She did the Will of God as it was made known to her from moment to moment. She obeyed. And never forget, that, since God is God, every new moment is for you another greeting by Gabriel, another "annunciation," another manifestation of what God wants from you *now*.

There will be a temptation to negate all this about Mary by saying: "She was conceived immaculate; I was born in sin." That is true. But just remember what happened to you at baptism. You were "born of God." You were given everything you need for your career. You have been as amply supplied with the necessary tools for your work as was Mary for hers. You have been given a share in God's own nature; you have a free will that has been made powerful enough to effect by a *Fiat* all that the omnipotent God desires from you. But the point was that there is ordinariness about mystery and there is matter-of-factness about saving mankind. You yourself are a mystery — and you will ever live and move in the mysteries of God. You are a "sacrament" — a sacred sign, a visible means of invisible grace. You are a savior. And all this by the Will of God. Like Mary, though in a lower degree, you are to be coredeemer; but you will never be what you are unless, like her, you make an unconditional surrender to God; that is total commitment of self to the lone Sovereign; that is wedding human will to the divine. That is the only way to save yourself — or others.

But never forget that in all outward appearances Mary was as ordinary after that *Fiat* as she was before it. So if your life seems very ordinary, rejoice!

It is mysterious, no one can deny. Yet some solution to the mystery is given by St. Paul when he says to the Corinthians: "Just consider your own call, brothers; not many of you were wise, not many influential, not many noble by worldly standards. But God chose what the world holds foolish, to put to shame the wise, and what the world holds weak God chose to put to shame the mighty, and what the world holds ignoble and despicable, and what counts for nought God chose, to bring to nought the things that count . . ." (1 Cor. 1:26–28). So if you feel yourself and really are considered by the world to be unwise, ignoble, without influence, weak, and to be despised, know that you are the very one God selects. "From him comes your union in Christ Jesus, who has become for us God-given wisdom and holiness and sanctification and redemption" (1 Cor. 1:29, 30).

You save the world "in Christ Jesus" — and you save it no other way. He told you so Himself: "One bears abundant fruit only when he and I are mutually united; severed from me, you can do nothing" (Jn. 15:5). But we are united to Him; for we are His members. That is why we can save the world by doing God's Will in our ordinary daily tasks; for each is an "annunciation" of what God would have us do for Him and His Christ. Each has his appointed share in the one work. Paul put it thus to his Ephesians: "He (Christ) established some men as apostles, and some as inspired spokesmen, others again as evangelists, and others as pastors and teachers, thus organizing the saints for the work of the ministry, which consists in building up the body of Christ, until we all attain to unity in faith and deep knowledge of the Son of God. Thus we attain to perfect manhood, to the mature proportions that befit Christ's complement" (Eph. 4:11–13). There again is another statement of your God-given career: you are to attain to perfect manhood, the mature proportions that befit Christ.

That babe in arms, that teen-ager, that young man making love, that wife and mother, that truck driver, that paperboy and boot-black, that governor and senator, as well as that priest and prelate are all one in Christ thanks to baptism, and each holds his appointed place by God's Will for one ultimate purpose: that maturity which befits the Body of Jesus Christ. So let us realize intensely that "there is a distribution of gifts, but the same Spirit distributes them. There is a distribution of ministrations, but it is the same Lord to whom we minister. There is a distribution of activities, but it is the same God who activates them all in everyone" (1 Cor. 12:4–7). That explains both your position and your power in God's plan. You are where you are, and you have the gifts, ministry and activity that are yours simply because God so willed it. You cannot fail in your career if you will only realize two things: (1) it is simple and (2) you are not alone.

Paul has more elucidation of you and your position for you in this same Epistle and this same chapter. He says:

> For example, just as the body is a unit, although it has many members, and all the members of the body, many though they are, form but one body, so too is the Christ. . . . As it is, God has put the members, every last one of them, in the body, as he wished. . . . As it is, there are certainly many members, but a unified body. The eye cannot say to the hand, "I have no need of you," nor the head to the feet, "I have no need of you." On the contrary, much rather are those members of the body necessary, which seem the weakest. . . . You are Christ's body and individually its members. And God has established in his Church some in the first rank, namely apostles, others in the second rank . . ." (1 Cor. 12:12 ff.).

Society is stratified. The Church is hierarchical. The Mystical Body has many members. But each has his own work to do for the building up of that Body, which is the real reason for the existence of mankind on earth this moment. You have a God-given career. It is to help the Father accomplish the "re-establishment of everything in Christ" through the Holy Spirit. That is God's Will in general. Now to look at it in particular. . . .

CHAPTER EIGHT

"IF I ONLY KNEW GOD'S WILL FOR ME... RIGHT NOW!"

Just as it is only the fool who says there is no God, so it is only the greatest fool who would refuse to do God's Will. Ordinary men are not fools. But, while giving sincere affirmation to each of the conclusions so far reached, while readily accepting the general thesis about life's purpose, while being ready and even anxious to do God's Will – and do it with generosity – there are those who say they are never sure what God's Will is for them. That should never be!

On Sinai God expressed His Will for every man – and had it written in stone. Those Ten Commandments are never fully understood until they are seen to be one. God's Will for you in time and for all eternity can be expressed in three monosyllables. St. John told us that "God is Love." The Ten Commandments can be expressed in the one: *Thou shalt love.* That is the command that is to rule you not only now but forever.

The finger of God traced out three commands on one half of the stone Moses brought down from Sinai. Those three are one: *Thou shalt love God.* The second half of the stone holds seven laws that have to do with love for yourself and love for your neighbor. The Fourth Commandment is a law of love between child and parents. The remaining six commands tell us different ways of loving ourselves and our fellow humans. Every thunderous "Thou shalt not . . ." can be stated positively; and all can be summed up in the one: "Thou shalt love."

The thing we are to remember is that these Ten Commandments bind us twenty-four hours a day. Hence, there is never a split second when we do not know God's Will in our own regard. He wills that we be creatures of love; that we manifest our love all the day long, then on through the night. He wills that we love Him, ourselves, and all our fellows all the time. Of course bulky volumes have been written on these Commandments, showing how they fan out to cover every situation of our lives and every relation with God, self, and others that can ever be encountered. But we live only one moment at a time, and we encounter only one set of circumstances at a time. Hence, the art of living reduces itself to the art of loving. If man would learn to live right, let him learn to love.

It was St. Bernard of Clairvaux who said: "The highest of all arts is the art of love." This outstanding Cistercian monk wrote a whole treatise on love, telling its nature and its dignity. He became a monk, then reached his towering stature among monks, only because he was a great lover. We have debased the word "love" to such an extent that some hesitate to use it without some adjective such as "pure" or "true." But there never was, nor will there ever be, any love that is not both true and pure; for "love takes its origin in God" (1 Jn. 4:7).

Another great lover, and another great saint precisely because he was so great a lover, Francis de Sales, once exclaimed: "Poor souls! They torment themselves about finding the art of loving God, and they do not know that there is none but to love Him." We learn by doing. If we would learn the art of loving, we must love.

Babies need no tutors to show them how to love their mothers and fathers. It is as natural for them to love as it is to breathe. Then why should we grown-up babies find it other than natural for us to love Him from whom we have been born again? You may say that a child's love is an instinctive thing, without reason, and very much of the flesh. But that is only to condemn us "children of a larger growth"; for we are supposed to have reason, to recognize what is good in our instincts, and to rise above the flesh. The truth remains: *Solvitur ambulando* — "We learned to walk by walking"; we will learn to love by loving. It will not be as slow nor as painful a lesson as was walking. If we should at first feel awkward, let us persevere; gracefulness will soon be ours.

The eloquent Lacordaire once said: "*I love you.* Ten thousand words may precede these, but none follows in any language; and when we have spoken them to someone, there is only one other recourse — to repeat them forever. The tongue of man can go no further, because his heart does not go beyond this point."

God Himself has told us how to say "I love You" to Him. It is St. John who gives us the report. It was during His farewell discourse that Christ said: "He who accepts my commandments and treasures them — he is the one that loves me" (Jn. 14:21). Then this Man Jesus, who is God and Truth Incarnate, immediately added a proof that "as we sow so shall we reap," that if we sow love we will reap love, and even the increase one expects at harvest after a generous sowing; for Christ said: "And he that loves me will, in turn, be loved by my Father; and I will love him, and will manifest myself to him" (*ibid.*).

It was in the warm, friendly intimacy of this Last Supper, an intimacy that was shot through and through with the deepest emotions in the human heart of God, that Jesus showed us another way of saying "I love You, God." It came after Christ's own protestations of love. He had been saying: "Just as the Father loves me, so I love you." Then He went on begging for human love: "Be sure to hold my love," He said. "If you treasure my commandments you will hold my love. . . . This is my commandment: love one another as I love you. . . . This is all I command you: love one another" (Jn. 15:9–17). And this strong, almost pleading repetition came quite some moments after He had first said: "A new commandment I give you: love one another; as I love you, so I want you, too, to love one another. By this token all the world must know that you are my disciples — by cherishing love for one another" (Jn. 13:34, 35).

Now let God the Holy Spirit speak to you through the instrumentality of St. Paul. Writing to his Romans, this great lover gave us these lines:

> Let there be no unpaid debt except the debt of mutual love, because he who loves his neighbor has fulfilled the Law. For the commandments:

> You shall not commit adultery;
> You shall not kill;
> You shall not steal;
> You shall not covet;
>
> and if there is any other commandment, all are summed up in this saying:
>
> "You shall love your neighbor as yourself."
>
> Love does no evil to a neighbor. Love, therefore, is the complete fulfillment of the Law (Rom. 13:8–10).

Later the same Holy Spirit, treating the same truth and theme, spoke through the last living Apostle, St. John the Beloved:

> Beloved, I am not writing you a new commandment, but the old one, which you have heard from the beginning. The old commandment is the message which you have heard. And yet, it is a new commandment I write to you, new in regard to him and in regard to you, because the darkness is passing away, and the true light is already shining. He who says that he is in the light, yet hates his brother, is still in darkness. He who loves his brother abides in the light . . . (1 Jn. 2:7–10).

Does that stir up memories of other passages from this same St. John? He is the Evangelist of Light and Life and Love. He told you that Christ is the Light of the world and that you are also the world's real light; that you are to abide in Christ and Christ in you; that you are children of light and the very offspring of Love. The entire First Epistle of St. John will make rewarding reading for anyone and everyone at any time and every time. But right now what we want to ponder is this passage:

> God is love, and he who abides in love abides in God and God in him. This love has become perfect through our cooperation. . . . If anyone says, "I love God," yet hates his brother, he is a liar. Why? Because he who does not love his brother whom he sees, cannot love God whom he does not see. Besides, we have received this commandment from God: He who loves God must love his brother also (1 Jn. 4:16–21).

John could never forget the way Christ had silenced the Pharisees when one of their legal experts tried to trap Jesus with the question: "Rabbi, which is the great commandment in the Law?" The Son of God knew what was in this man's heart, so He replied: " 'Love the Lord your God with your whole heart, and with your whole soul, and with your whole mind.' This is the great and first commandment. But a second commandment is like it: 'Love your neighbor as yourself.' On these two commandments hinge the whole Law and the Prophets" (Mt. 22:37–40). That is why John could write so confidently: "We know that we have passed from death to life, because we love our brothers. He who does not love abides in death" (1 Jn. 3:14).

Before him St. Matthew had written: "If you want to enter eternal life, keep the commandments" (Mt. 19:17). And Luke had written in the same strain, using the words of Jesus just as Matthew had done. They form a preamble to the parable of the Good Samaritan; for a legal expert again had tried to trap Him with the question: "Rabbi, what must I do to obtain a place in eternal life?" Jesus asked him to quote the Law. The man did, giving the two commandments on love. Jesus said to him: "Your answer is correct; act accordingly, and you will have life" (Lk. 10:25–28).

So the Will of God is clear enough for any of us. We must love. But we must always remember that love is shown by deeds rather than words: "Let us not love merely in word or with the tongue, but in *action* and *reality*" (1 Jn. 3:18). "To love God means to keep his commandments" (1 Jn. 5:3).

There are those in our day who know the Will of God and do it. The Abbé Pierre, founder of "the Ragpickers of Emmaus," the man who by one radio appeal in Paris let loose what has been termed an "insurrection of kindness" and who has gone on to found an international association with "Serve the neediest first" as its law of laws, is one twentieth-century man who takes the parable of the Good Samaritan quite literally and the command of Christ to love most personally. He has said that "when one is tending the weakest of mankind, then he is in the hand of the All-Powerful, and is part of His most urgent Will." When writing on this command to love he asked: "Is it a new commandment?" and answered: "Yes, because every day, for us, everything is new in the objectives which have never ceased to beckon us forward: the Good, the True, and the Right. It is an unremitting commandment, which no one who hears it can ever forget. It is the Law of laws."

He did not hesitate to say that "the law of God is perfectly plain, and if we forget it, the law of events, the law of the centuries, the brutal law of historical consequences will be certain to jog our memories. . . . There have been great empires in the past, peoples who enjoyed fantastic wealth. What remains of all that today? Read a little history, and you will find the answer. The peoples whose might has been reduced to nothing and who today are no more than a wretched and contemptible remnant, didn't *know how to love,* they weren't able to observe the Law."

He concluded this argument with the stirring words: "We believe that God is Love, and we believe that He will judge us. Don't let us ever forget what He has told us and solemnly repeated. He will judge us by the extent to which our Faith and our religious practice have inspired us to love those who suffer more than we do. He will expect us to serve them before ourselves as long as they are suffering more than we, even though it means a sacrifice." Lest that have too depressing a coloring, let me add that the Abbé also said: "The extraordinary weeks of the 'insurrection of kindness,' and the exhausting but wonderful years I've lived through since then have convinced me of one thing. They have convinced me that one day soon a spark is going to be struck which will kindle all over the world an *active love* of men for each other."*

The secret of Abbé Pierre's life and love is that he believes in Jesus Christ and in the plan of the Father to "re-establish all things in Christ." He knows the Will of God right now. He knows that we should *love.* He hears God crying, " 'I'm hungry, I'm thirsty, I'm deserted, I'm in pain . . .' through a million million human voices. . . ."

This man received no more revelation than did you or I. The difference is that he believes; too many of us only profess to believe. He knows that love serves; too many of us think that love speaks ear-tickling and heart-warming words. He knows the command of God and he fulfills it; too many of us go on repeating: "If I only knew God's Will in my regard. . . ."

It is true that we no longer have patriarchs like Abraham, Isaac,

---

* *Man is Your Brother* (Westminster, Md.: Newman, 1958), pp. 3 and 86.

and Jacob; that we are without leaders like Moses, Aaron, and Josue; that the Prophets are long since silent. But we have the voice of Him who raised up the patriarchs and leaders of the people, the voice of Him who inspired the Prophets; and that voice speaks to us with a clarity that allows for no confusion. We have the Word of God speaking to us through His vicars, the popes. The Will of God has been made manifest to us through encyclicals and addresses; so clearly manifest that no man can say he is without *divine* directive in any of the problems of the day.

But some may still object and say that they yet crave something more immediate, more personal, more definitely touching them in their individual circumstances at the present moment. Of course one could remind them that what is called the "voice of conscience" is actually the voice of God; that it is the law of God, the Will of God, and ultimately a demand that they love. But to make the Will of God as personal and private as their own name, we appeal not to conscience but to consciousness.

Why are you where you are at this moment? Why have you your position, profession, or job? Why are you in the class you are in: married or unmarried? Why are you a member of the Church to which you belong? Why are you doing what you are doing at this very moment?

Now you may start with your birth from your specific parents to account for your present station in life, and tell of your inherited tendencies and your acquired abilities. You may speak of relatives, connections, and even of pure "chance" or "accident"; of environment and education, good friends and evil ones, good "breaks" and bad ones. But you can sum it all up in the one word: God.

You are what you are, and you are where you are, in the condition, social stratum, economic rating, and cultural grouping simply because God so willed it. There is no one in the world, from prime ministers and presidents down to peasants and prisoners, who is not what he is and where he is simply because God has so decreed.

You will admit that God *foresaw* that you would be what you are, where you are, and doing what you are doing this very moment — and foresaw it from all eternity. You will also have to admit that you would not be just what you are and where you are, and doing what you are doing right now had God not *foreordained* it. Of course, if you are not in His friendship, and pulsing with His divine life, then you are in the condition you are by what is called His permissive Will. But the fact remains that you and everyone else are doing what you and they are doing, and in the position you and they are at this moment only by the Will of God. So no man can say with any truth that he does not know the Will of God in his regard this very second. In whatever position you find yourself you *now* know that God wants you to love Him, yourself, and your neighbor. You know that this is not to be merely affective love, but God wills that you put forth a love that is effective.

Employers have never been noted, as a group, for any demonstrativeness toward their employees. But if you are an employer and you want to know the Will of God in your regard, be certain that He wills that you show an effective love toward each and every one in your employ. He has told you this through the pens of Leo XII and Pius XI. He had these two vicars of His Son write encyclicals on labor that will live as long as there are men who will labor — and that, despite all the advances and devices in technology, will be as long as there are men. Effective love gives a wage that is in all truth a "living wage" — not a wage that will enable one to eke out an existence; not a "sustaining wage" — but a wage that will enable a man, his wife, and his family to *live*. Before any man can be said to live aright he must have the wherewithal to enjoy some leisure amid a modicum of what are called luxuries.

If anyone is looking for an answer to Karl Marx's *Das Kapital*, and, in point of fact, to communism and socialism no matter what their particular form, let him read Leo XIII's *Rerum Novarum*. That was written in 1891 but contains the Will of God for us right now. "As a general rule," says the Pontiff, "a workman ought to have leisure and rest proportionate to the wear and tear of his strength; for waste of strength must be repaired by cessation from hard work. In agreements between masters and work-people there is always the condition expressed or understood, that there should be allowed proper rest for soul and body. To agree in any other sense would be . . . giving up those duties which a man owes to his God and to himself."

The same Pope expresses the Will of God for all those employed when he wrote: "If a workman's wages be sufficient to enable him to maintain himself, his wife, and his children in reasonable comfort, he will not find it difficult, if he is a sensible man, to study economy; and he will not fail, by cutting down expenses, to put by some little savings and thus secure a small income."

His Holiness used the term "reasonable comfort" in place of the "modicum of luxuries" employed above. But the idea expressed is the same. God wants all peoples to know leisure, relaxation, recreation, and the peace of mind that comes from a sense of security. All can be had if the employer grants the *living* wage and the employee *lives within it!*

But in this age of supersonic speeds we squander just about everything: we squander time, strength of body, both in sports and at work; we squander strength of mind in dealing with trivialities, nonessentials, and nonproductives; we squander our few savings and much of our earnings living beyond our incomes; we squander our leisure; we squander our lives. We may well be squandering our eternity. God's Will is that we be not squanderers.

That is why He had Pius XI repeat the teachings of Leo XIII in the *Quadragesimo Anno.* Men have hailed these two encyclicals as the productions of creative geniuses and seized upon certain phrases, repeating them so often and so strongly that some have come to accept them as adequate summaries of the Catholic Church's teaching. Thus we have heard the virtues of justice and charity extolled, and by adding an adjective to them, a rallying cry has been born. Now it is true that both Pontiffs insisted on social justice and social charity. But careful reading and proper thinking will show all that underlying the papal directives is recognition of divine providence ever operative in our economy, and a call on all men — employees and employers — to use that first and most important cardinal virtue of *prudence.*

Banish the idea that this virtue is for the timid or the temporizer! This "pilot of the virtues," as St. Thomas called it, is for the bold, the prompt, the vigorous. It is the virtue of the practical man, the doer; but before it allows him to be the doer, it makes him the thinker; for prudence is the virtue by which a man selects and orders means to an end, and foresees the results that will come from his action. Therefore, the end must be known, and the plan ordering the selected means to that end must pre-exist in the mind of the practical man before he sets about his operation. But that is only another description of what we have called providence. In fact, the great St. Thomas has said: "The plan of things to be ordered to an end is, properly speaking, providence. It is the principal part of *prudence* to which two other parts are ordered in providing for future things: memory of things past, and understanding of things present." There you have the past, present, and future caught up in the now — and that shows you how we men of the moment share somehow in the eternality of God. We, by an exercise of prudence, participate in divine providence. There is such a thing, then, as human providence, which, in all actuality, is a sharing in the very providence of God. In the article cited above, St. Thomas Aquinas goes on to say that "human providence is contained under Divine Providence as a particular cause is contained under a universal Cause." As we have been insisting all along, God shares causality with His rational creatures. "The rational creature participates in Divine Providence not only in being governed but in governing. He governs himself in his own acts, and he governs other things also," is how St. Thomas put it. Hence, the imperative necessity for cultivating *prudence* at all times — for "providence is the principal part of prudence from which the virtue takes its name" (IIa IIae, q. 49, a. 6).

Belloc and Chesterton used to insist that the medieval man was the most modern of men. If this is true we can learn from this man of the thirteenth century how to act in the middle of the twentieth. He distinguished between personal, political, and economic prudence; then taught that wealth was not the ultimate end to be sought by economic prudence, but to be employed as a means to the ultimate end which is "total well-being in domestic living."

How many can tell what is meant by "total well-being in domestic living"? How many will see that simply as another means to their unqualified ultimate end: union with God, a share in His holiness, peace, happiness? Those who have clear concepts as to their purpose in life know that the one virtue they must cultivate constantly is the one which enables them to keep human providence working hand in hand with divine providence — and that virtue is prudence.

They will realize that the wages from work are given by God not to enable them to "keep up with the Joneses" — but to be employed with such prudence that they may catch up to Christ; for they know the Will of God in their regard, and recognize economic life as but another phase of their religious living. They have integrated their existence here on earth; for they know that if they are to make something worthwhile out of themselves and all their days they must do what God wants done — and that is what Christ did: the Will of the Father every hour of the day. For them, going to work on a weekday is as important to their mission in life as going to church on Sunday; for it contributes to that only ultimate: the glorification of God and the sanctification of men, just as really, in its way, as does the observance of the Lord's Day. For them it is but another form of worship; for it is but another form of obedience to God's Will. They know they must have money; and they earn it. But it is not for the sake of amassing a fortune; it is simply to be faithful to God and co-operate with Him in His providence.

The Will of God is that we always "walk in the newness of life" (Rom. 6:4). That "newness" is to permeate our entire living: economic, social, domestic, personal, private, public, and liturgical. Perhaps that last word tells us all. For the one *Leiturgos* of all time was and is Jesus Christ. He, the Second Person of the Trinity, became a Man and, as a Man, performed the one public action that satisfied Divinity for all the people. That public action was His Mass: the Cenacle, Calvary, the empty tomb, the ascent from Olivet's top, the enthronement at the Father's right. To offer that Mass was the real purpose of His life and living. That is why He was sent into the world. That is why we are still in this world. Liturgy is life when we understand the word in the fullness of its most living meaning. The Will of God for the ordinary man is that he be Christ; that he live "by a new principle of life" — we call it Grace. It is a share in the very life of God. It was won for us by Christ through His Liturgical Act — the Mass. Hence, if we Christians are to live aright we must always be living the Mass, which means being "alive to God in Christ Jesus" (Rom. 6:11). Which, in its turn, means being alive to God, alive with God, alive in God, alive for God every living moment. Therefore, we must be "saying our Mass" even as we stand by some machine in a factory, plow the earth as a farmer, dig in the bowels of the earth as a miner, examine the things of earth in a laboratory, store the things of earth in a warehouse, or prepare the things of earth for sale in some market or for consumption at some table. It makes no difference where we work, or at what we work, the Will of God for each of us now is that our work be offered as "bread and wine" to be "transubstantiated" into acceptable reparation, thanksgiving, adoration, and impetration. Work can be, and is meant by God to be, liturgical; and you, the worker, will be prudent only if you realize that you are always a liturgist. Work means wages, it is true; but it is even truer that work should always mean worship. For such is the will of God for you.

It is Jean Guitton who says: "a Fifth Gospel exists. It lies open in every man. It is his poor human life, since Christ is there."

Have you been a living Gospel? Have you radiated Christ at all times, in all places, to all peoples? Have you taught the Way, the Truth, and the Life to everyone who came within the orbit of your living by the manner in which you walked the Way, told the Truth, and lived the Life? If not, you have been imprudent and improvident; you have not been doing the Will of God; for you have not *loved.*

"Greater love than this," said Christ, "no man has. . . ." Then He went out from the Cenacle to the Garden; from the Garden to the various courts; from the courts to Calvary; from Calvary to the tomb; from the tomb back to the Cenacle, the road to Emmaus, Tiberias' Lake, and finally back to the Father. "Greater love than this — " is the Mass. If you have not been living the Mass all your live-long day and night, you have not been loving; you have not been living.

Do not turn from this page with the thought: "That is to think like and live like a mystic." For make no mistake about it: God made you to be a mystic. The mistake our age has made is to think that Christ's Mass consists entirely in what happened on Calvary, and to identify Christianity with suffering. Such an aberration leads to veiled Manichaeism. Christ was doing the Will of the Father and, consequently, saving mankind in Bethlehem, Egypt, Nazareth, all Judea, Samaria just as well as in Jerusalem or just outside its walls; He was glorifying God as he dined sumptuously with Simon the Pharisee, Levi the tax collector, and Zacchaeus just as really as when He had to change water into wine or multiply loaves and fishes; He was meriting life for you and me as He enjoyed Himself with Martha, Mary, and Lazarus just as effectively as when soldiers struck Him in the face, buffeted Him and spat upon His sacred features. Everything that Christ did, everything that Christ touched, everything that Christ experienced was somehow made divine. And if we will be Christians we must come to recognize the divine in all that is human. Since the Incarnation, not only our flesh, but everything connected with our humanity, has been changed. Since joy, hunger, sleep, suffering, friendship, banqueting, rest, thirst, and all the others have been assumed by a divine Person, it follows that all our human conditions have had a sacred value imparted to them. Please understand that fully. It does not mean that these human things became somewhat divine only when Christ assumed them, but *now* when every Christian has part in them. The Will of God is that we be always offering "bread and wine" to Him. Those essential elements for the Mass are to be found by employer and employee in work and wages, success and failure, profit and loss, labor and leisure. Both he who hires and he who is hired must be mystics or be written off as human mistakes. According to the Will of God there is no other alternative. *Non datur tertium,* St. Thomas would say — "There is no third term!"

How simple it is for an ordained priest to say Mass. How easy! He bends over bread and wine and speaks five or six words, and it is accomplished! "All is consummated!" Why so easy for a mortal to bring about a miracle? Why so simple a thing as breathing a few words above a host and a chalice to effect something so surpassingly sublime? Because God is God and the priest, at that moment, is Christ in the Cenacle, on Calvary, and at the right hand of the Father.

It is no more complicated or difficult for the owner or the worker to live his "Mass" in the economic milieu; for he, too, is Christ. He, too, if baptized and confirmed, shares in Christ's own priesthood. He may not consecrate; but he must offer. He must present God with elements to be "transubstantiated." It is as easy as breathing. No more difficult than whispering a few meaningful words. But it is as sublime as Christ; as holy as God.

If workers and those who employ them are alert they have learned from the Worker-Priests of France, and the suppression of that movement by the Holy See, that they, the laymen, must be that Fifth Gospel Guitton speaks about; must make holy, with the holiness of God, the work they do and the place in which they do it.

What has just been said about employer and employee is true not only about the husband and father who leaves the house each day to earn his living but also of the woman who, as wife and mother, stays home to clean the house and care for the children. She, too, shares in Christ's priesthood. Consequently, the Will of God for her right now is that she be Christ; that her life be liturgy; that she hold out wheat in the paten of her hands and offer wine from the chalice of her heart every day, all the day long, and then on into the night. For each human life, no matter where lived, or in what position passed, has but one goal: God. And God, of course, is to be adored the way He wills to be adored: by the Mass in every now of time.

Not enough women realize that their kitchen floor can be for them and their loved ones what the threshing floor of Areuna became for David and his people — a place of sacrifice. It is there that David offered sacrifice and thus saved his people (cf. 2 Kgs. 24). Hence it is that the kitchen floor is the place where God wills that housewives offer Him sacrifice. All they need do is realize that by sweeping that floor as part of their day's work as wife and mother, they are working hand in hand with God. They are exercising human providence as part of divine providence. They are pleasing the Lord God of heaven and earth even as did His only Son; for they are doing His Will for them in the now.

Modern women must look on all things in their pantry and kitchen as St. Benedict bids the cellarer to look on all the goods of the monastery: "as if they were the sacred vessels of the altar"

(Ch. 31). Every housewife must come to consider her house as holy as the sanctuary, and herself as specially selected by God to serve Him there. Married women must become keenly conscious of the fact that they live in a "sacramental *state*," that holiness becomes their house since it is a "house of God." Small wonder they feel frustrated, confused; and their lives disintegrated. They think that the Church — that material building which is their gathering place on Sunday — is the only "house of God" in their vicinity; and that it is only there, on the consecrated altar, that sacrifice is to be offered to God. Naturally that fragments their existence; for God is the Source of all existence, and if they turn fully to the Source only in Church it is no wonder they are somewhat bewildered the rest of the week. If a helpless child turned to its mother or father only once a week, what would happen to it? We are children of God — and very helpless children at that. The Will of God for each of us right now is that we should grow up — in Him, for Him, and even like Him. There is only one way of doing that. By constant contact with Him. That continual contact can be had, should be had, and, one may dare say, *must* be had in the state of life in which we live, and through the duties of that state.

There is another of those sacred words which we moderns must rediscover, and to which we must allow that deep existence from which alone it can produce those resonances we need to hear in order to understand its loveliness — and to come to love it. The moment we hear the word "duty," too many of us grimace and slump at the shoulders. That reaction comes simply because we have reduced this word, which is thunderous with the sound of God and eternity, to a "thin trickle of sound."

Have you ever thought of duty as the most ennobling thing about your existence? That is one of its first meanings. It refers to that which is "becoming." What makes a man a man? Certainly not physical stature. Just as certainly not intellectual acumen. Manhood lies much deeper. It lies in doing what is "becoming." Father Gerald Vann, O.P., has put it concisely: *Morals* maketh man.

Again we are forced to have recourse to semantics. What reactions are set up by that word "moral"? Do not most moderns immediately think of the Puritans and prudishness? But that is sheer stupidity; for morals make a man a man and not a caricature of one. Philosophy defines man as a "rational animal." It is a good definition especially when, by association of ideas, it calls up that quip of Mark Twain about man being rational in definition more often than in real life. But we can also quite correctly define man as a "religious animal" — and consequently, just as accurately and adequately as a "moral animal." A good definition, the ancients used to say, will apply to *all* the members of the thing defined, *always* to each of them, and *only* to them. Man is the only creature who rationalizes, the only visible creature on earth who is religious, and consequently the only being on earth who can be and should be moral. Let it be said once again: Morals make a man . . . and a woman; and nothing else really does!

It is our duty to be moral. It is "becoming." When you tell a pretty girl (and, *a fortiori,* one who is not so pretty) that her hair-do or her hat is "becoming," you will see no slump in her shoulders or any grimace about her mouth. Hence, one might say that it is the duty of every woman to look right. When you tell a growing boy or a fully adult man that his actions are "becoming," neither will sag or slouch. For way down deep they know it is their duty to do right. Now if there is propriety about looking right and doing right, what shall we say about that duty incumbent on every man, woman, and child to *be* right? That is what it means to be moral — or in other words what it means to be human.

That takes us one step further and brings us to another magnificent word: *obligation.*

When you say of a man or a woman that he or she is "a very obliging person," what a volume of praise you have uttered. How is it, then, that from the same root we have such different flowers? such different fruits? If "obligingness" makes a person so acceptable and worthy of warm praise, why should not "obligations" make all men and women, and even little children, outstandingly superior beings? They do. For the fact is that just as we compliment a person by calling him "obliging," God has complimented us stupendously by laying on us "obligations." It "becomes" us to be "obliging" to God. It is our highest duty; our most distinguishing prerogative. Fulfilling it makes us just.

We build our human lives "four-square" only when we build them on the four moral virtues of justice, temperance, fortitude, and prudence. If we were pressed to name the most essential of those four, unquestionably most of us would pick out justice. Nor would we be far wrong. For all that we have been considering about duty, obligations, morality, and true manhood is directly connected with this one virtue. And when we are just, we give to each what is his due, beginning, of course, with God.

Some modern sophisticates, even in the spiritual world, would make of religion the service of God to man. They write and speak as if God existed and is to be courted for what He can do for man. They have devised some peculiar sort of spirituality which is not only personal and individual but even purely subjective. God is God, and if we humans will be human, we will not use Him, but let Him use us. We will be just. We will do our duty. We will fulfill our obligations. We will do what is becoming — becoming to God and becoming to His rational, religious, moral beings. We will be objective!

Not many sons of Adam or daughters of Eve are consistently objective. What happened in Eden makes each of us very selfish and almost continually inclined to be pronouncedly subjective. We are loud in our demands for justice; crying always for what we consider *our* due. But too seldom are we objective enough to consider first what is due to God, then, later, what is due to others. Justice is a cardinal virtue, that is, a virtue on which much hinges; but most of us need to oil those hinges which are rusty from lack of use.

Yet it is this virtue that makes a man most moral and most a man. Do we not hail the just man as the "upright" man, and a man of "integrity"? For decades of years now the would-be experts on human well-being, the psychologists and psychiatrists, have been asking for what they call "integration." Here it is for them in a form few of them will recognize, and fewer still accept and utilize. Justice, the paying to God, to self, and to others what is due, will integrate the life of any man and every man. It will make him whole — an Anglo-Saxon word which means sound and healthy, and is kin to that other Anglo-Saxon word *halig* from which we get our telling word "holy." What a cascade of truths now tumbles out on us:

if a man will be a man he must be moral; if he is moral he will do what is becoming, always act obligingly, and ever be just; if he is just he will be whole — sane, sound, healthy; if he is whole he will be holy. The real man, then, is not only sane, he is saintly.

To be what we are, then, we have but to fulfill the duties of our state in life. That will be justice; that will be morality; that will make us obliging, and make us do what is most becoming — namely, the Will of God in the now.

The phrase that set us off unraveling so much that modern sophisticates and superficial thinkers have snarled up by their carelessness with words and their deep meanings was "duties of that state" — and we were considering the marriage state, which is a sacramental state. A state is a permanent form of existence. So long as the marriage lasts, its every second is sacramentalized; hence, one is justified in talking to husbands and wives, mothers and fathers of each new *now* as a "sacrament."

A sacrament is a "visible sign instituted by Christ to give grace." That is a real definition. But since grace is the life of God granted to man, we will not be wrong to say that a sacrament is a coming of God to man to fill him more fully with life that is divine. That is an acceptable definition of every new now in the life not only of each married man and woman, but of every woman and man. But sacraments must be received before they can bear fruit. If we do not recognize God in each new now, realizing it is a gift, a grace which holds seed for glory, we are not doing His Will, we are not just, obliging, moral, or fully human. We are not doing our duty — which in ultimate analysis is to grow and grow more like God — a thing which can be done only by grace, which is sharing ever more fully in His life.

Henri Bergson was not a Catholic. He did not die in the Church established by Christ. But as the hour of his death approached, he was on the threshold. Why he did not cross it is a mystery that must await solution in eternity. But that he was a thinker no one will deny. He had almost plumbed the depths of man when he said there is in every human being "an urge which bears him toward God"; and Bergson almost entered into mysticism when he called that "urge" a "never-satisfied movement."

You will never satisfy that urge this side of the face-to-face vision of God. But you can come closer and closer to satisfaction by receiving God in the "sacrament" of each new now. That is His Will for you, for me, for every human being on earth. And if we know ourselves for what we really are, it will be our will, too. Then we will be in love; for what is the meeting of two wills but supreme love and ecstatic loving. So we are back to our old proposition: it is our duty to love, since it is our privilege to live. For God is Love, and we are "born of God."

Never need you say you are not sure of God's Will in your regard; for it lies in the duty of the present moment in the state in which you find yourself in this passing *now*.

Take your ordinary day. You wake. God wills that you awake as any parent wills that his child awakes. As the child becomes conscious he or she will focus on you, slowly recognize you, and smile. We are children of God no matter what our chronological age or physical development. He can but will as any parent wills: that we wake up, see Him bending over us, recognize Him, and smile our love and appreciation of life.

Of course there are days when any child awakes with a frown. But even then there is recognition of the parent who has awakened him, and there is some sort of greeting. We older children of God awake occasionally "out of sorts." Nevertheless it is God's Will that we greet Him. Bishop Sheen is fond of repeating two possible greetings that can fall from our lips as we become conscious each new day. It is either: "Good morning, God" – or "Good God, morning!" Even when we wake "out of sorts" we can make that second greeting a prayer by emphasizing the first word and not the last. God is good when He grants us a new day – no matter how we feel on finding that it is ours. It is a sacramental moment for all who live in a sacramental state. It is a moment for sacrament for everyone no matter what his state – even if it be a state of sin. It is a new *now* – and God wills that we receive Him in it.

The clothing of our bodies, the adorning of our persons, the food and drink we take, the ride to work or the care we are to give the home – all is meant by God to be prayer and praise of Him, and a contribution to our mounting perfection as His children. In each new *now* we are to do what is "becoming," to see and recognize what we *ought:* Christ in every person, God in every event.

In his play *Murder in the Cathedral,* T. S. Eliot speaks of

> . . . the greatest treason:
> To do the right deed for the wrong reason.

That is why it is so essential that we begin our day with the right reason, that is, that we direct all our thoughts, words, deeds, actions, and operations to God — and to God alone. For we can too often do the "right deed for the wrong reason." If we wake, shower, dress meticulously, breakfast wisely, then head for work for any other reason than because each is the Will of God for us, we are guilty of treason; for we have not only betrayed God, we have betrayed ourselves — and others, inasmuch as we have not directed our acts so that they might glorify God and win grace for ourselves and our fellow man. For it is not what we humans do that counts, but only what we do humanly. No act of ours is a human act unless it proceed from intellect and will; unless it be motivated and directed; unless it be free. Hence, if our day with its succession of God-laden moments is to be anything more than a passage of time, it must be freely, consciously, deliberately offered to God. The intention is the soul of every human action. To say that "hell is paved with good intentions" is far more erroneous than to say that the "end justifies the means." One may head for hell if what he calls "intention" is nothing more than a concept connected with a limp, lifeless, sighing wish. But if that intention is good enough to spark his will to some sort of fire and he acts on it, he will never see hell's fire.

St. Lawrence Justinian has given us the directive in this matter when he writes: "Whoever is desirous of salvation must look to his intention in all his works, and direct his will to that which the Will of God directs, lest the sweat of his brow be all in vain. It profits little to carry out truly difficult enterprises, to be intimate with princes and kings, to acquire renown as saintly and wise, and to do all this with a *crooked* intention." How well T. S. Eliot has echoed the saint when he talks of "greatest treason." You need not be a religious or a priest to recognize the importance of the intention. Even the pagan Seneca realized it and wrote in one of his letters: "You sit at the bedside of your sick friend. Let us examine your motives. If you are seeking mention in his will, you are a vulture waiting for the corpse. For the one and same deeds can be vile or praiseworthy according to the intention for which they are done." St. Augustine has summed it up thus: it is "the good intention that makes the deed."

We will be wise to make the following morning offering upon getting out of bed:

My God, I offer Thee this day
All I shall think, or do, or say;
In union with what was done
On earth by Jesus Christ, Thy Son.

That will make of every moment of our day something that will live on in the endless now of eternity, not because we will think, or do, or say anything important this passing day, but the intention links us and our all to the Christ; and Jesus is of infinite worth. That bit of rhyme can mean more to God and to man than all human literature, for Augustine is right: "the good intention makes the deed."

The Apostleship of Prayer gives one a longer offering which renders things a bit more explicit perhaps. It offers all one's prayers, works, joys, and sufferings to Jesus "through the Immaculate Heart of Mary" and "in union with the Holy Sacrifice of the Mass throughout the world." That links us with Mary and the Mass. Stronger links neither God nor man can forge. And to be so linked is to live as God wills every man to live; for we are Christ's members, and Mary is Mother of us all. This particular morning offering goes on to specify the purposes for which we will pray, act, joy, and suffer this day as it says: "for all the intentions of Thy Sacred Heart, in reparation for my sins, for the intentions of all our associates . . ." Note how explicit love for God, for self, and for neighbor are made by that specification. But these three loves, which are really one, comprise the Will of God for every man in every now. So you see how "becoming" it is for us to begin our day with such a morning offering. There is high probability that, if we do, we shall go on in that day doing our duty, which consists in seeing Christ in every person, and finding God in every event.

Before any of us can do that with ease, grace, and perfection, we have to learn what Saul of Tarsus learned on the road to Damascus. That lesson is called the doctrine of the Mystical Body. It tells that Christ and Christians are but one Person – He, the Second Person of the Blessed Trinity. A truth so blinding and staggering had to be revealed in a blinding and staggering manner. Saul set out from Jerusalem ablaze with determination to hound every Christian man and woman to prison and to death. But when he returned to Jerusalem years later, it was as "an uncaught captive in the hands of Love." Saul was seeking Christians but it was the Christ who called out: "Saul, Saul, why do you persecute me?" Knocked from his horse, blinded by a heavenly light, the dumfounded zealot asked: "Who are you, Lord?" and heard the staggering reply: "I am Jesus, whom you are persecuting" (Acts 9:4, 5). It was the same voice that had questioned the guard in the high priest's house: ". . . why do you strike me?" (Jn. 18:23.) The conclusion is inescapable: the same Person suffered both blows – that from the guard, and those from Saul's persecution. With that bit of Revelation beating in our blood, it will not be difficult to recognize Christ in every human – but that Revelation must beat in our blood.

That makes it sound like a matter of life and death. Lest anyone take it differently, let him turn to St. Matthew's twenty-fifth chapter and read how God is to judge us. When John of the Cross said: "We shall be judged by love," some took it as something in the nature of a private revelation. But, no. John of the Cross simply summarized Christ's own description of the Last Judgment, a description which has shaken more than one; for it reveals the fact that it is not on our chastity that we will be judged, but on our charity. In other words, on love; and very precisely on our love of God as manifested in our love of Jesus Christ as He lives in our neighbor. . . . "For," says Christ, "I was hungry and you gave me to eat; I was thirsty, and you gave me to drink; I was a stranger, and you took me into your homes; I was naked, and you covered me; I was sick, and you visited me; I was in prison, and you came to see me." Like another Saul we will ask: "When did we see You hungry and feed You?" . . . The answer lies in the living of the doctrine of the Mystical Body of Christ; the doctrine it is our duty to learn — and live! For such is the Will of God.

So the man or woman awakes, makes an offering of his or her day, then goes about the business of living that offering. She will prepare breakfast for . . . Christ. She will then clear the table and do the dishes for . . . Christ. She will tidy her pantry and clean her house for . . . Christ. The mailman will come with nothing perhaps other than advertisements and bills. She will see in him and them . . . Christ. A Western Union boy may arrive with a wire that tells of the death of a loved one. She will see in him and the wire what John saw from his boat that night he and Peter and the others had gone fishing and caught nothing. With him she will say: "It is the Lord" (Jn. 21:7). And so on throughout the entire day she will see Christ in every person and find God in every event.

Again one anticipates the protest: "But that is to live like a mystic." And the only answer is: That is to live.

Maurice Zundel has remarked that "Religion is no specialized occupation; it is life which has been made divine." And an Abbé Pouget, who has been called "the modern Socrates," noted that "we do not say *Credo Deo,* that is, 'I believe in God's word'; nor even *Credo Deum* — 'I believe that God exists'; but *Credo* in *Deum.* The word '*in*' indicates a tendency — we give our *maximum.* That is full Religion." If we would do the Will of God right now, we will give our *maximum.* We will live as mystics; for we will do what we should do, do it well, and do it simply because it is the Will of God.

Were a mother and father to live as they ought, giving God their maximum, seeing Christ in one another, in their children, in all human beings, finding God in every event, toward and untoward, motivated by the one dynamic, the Will of God, their lives would speak to their children, their neighbors, and their entire milieu as did the prophets of old. Their actions would be eloquent with those vibrant and vibrating words: "God says . . ."

In Charles Péguy's long poem *God Speaks,* he tells how God speaks about sleep — that end of the ordinary day for the ordinary man:

I don't like the man who doesn't sleep, says God
Sleep is the friend of man.
Sleep is the friend of God
Sleep is perhaps the most beautiful thing I have created.
And I myself rested on the seventh day.
He whose heart is pure, sleeps
And he who sleeps has a pure heart.

That is the great secret of being as indefatigable as a child.
Of having the strength in the legs that a child has.
Those new legs, those new souls,
And to begin afresh every morning, ever new
Like young hope, new hope.

Péguy goes on to talk of the men who do not sleep and has God say:

I pity them. I am talking about those
who work and who, in this, obey my Commandment,
poor children, And who, on the other hand,
lack courage, lack confidence, and don't sleep.
I pity them. I have it against them. A little.
They won't trust me.
Like the child who innocently lies in his mother's arms,
thus do they not lie
Innocently in the arms of my Providence.*

So sleep too is the Will of God in your regard, hence, Paul was not spinning idle rhetoric nor multiplying words when he wrote: "Whether, then, you eat or drink, or do anything else, do everything for God's glory" (1 Cor. 10:31). So from morning unto night, then on through the night to the following dawn it is "becoming" to live *in* Christ and live *as* Christ, doing always the things that please the Father. That is living in love – which is God's Will for each of us not only in every new *now* but in eternity's *now* which is never renewed.

Married couples, to whom God has entrusted images of Himself, can, and are meant to, share in God's paternity and God's maternity – "never forgetting the children of their womb." Such is God's Will in their regard. But what of the unmarried? Can they say: "If I only knew God's Will. . . ."

* (New York: Pantheon Books, Inc., 1945), pp. 21–25.

CHAPTER NINE

EVERY BREATH... EVERY HEARTBEAT

One of the first surprises for a postulant or a novice in a religious order or community is the way time flies. If he analyzes the situation it almost immediately becomes evident that the days seem like hours, the weeks pass like days, and the months like weeks, because every hour of the day and night has its own particular assignment. The aspirant is so completely occupied, he has practically no opportunity to daydream; hence, the time does fly by. But of the many joys that come to such a beginner in the religious life none can compare with that which comes when he realizes that every split second of the day and night is not only given back to God, but given back according to His Will; that each and every breath, each and every heartbeat is offered to God the way He wants it; that his life can now be summed up as Christ's own was in the saying: "I do always the things that please him" (Jn. 8:29).

No delusion is possible here; for so long as the religious is living according to the Rule, every breath is drawn and every heartbeat is given under obedience to God's own Will. The truth in this tenet has been revealed by the Son of God. Jesus, speaking to the disciples, and consequently not only of them but of their lawful successors, said: "He who hears you, hears me" (Lk. 10:16). Therefore, when a religious receives a command from his immediate superior, that command, so long as it is within the Rule, can be taken as coming from the lips of God Himself. It is His Will made articulate. The same is true for the Rule itself; for this has been approved by the Sacred Congregation for Religious, which is but an extension of the mind, will, and voice of the Sovereign Pontiff, who, in his turn, is vicar and vice-gerent for God's own Son, who is "true God of true God." So the connections are strong and true. The superior is the "living voice" who interprets and commands according to the Rule; the Rule has been approved by competent authority in the Congregation; that authority is the Pope's own authority, which is the very authority of God as manifested in Jesus Christ.

The serious, deep-thinking aspirant will go one step further and know a joy that will never leave his soul, for it is a joy that rises from the fundamental truth of all human existence. Creaturehood for the rational being demands that each person love God with his whole heart, soul, mind, and strength of being throughout his unending existence. On earth creaturehood for the rational being demands that he come to know, and consequently to praise, revere, and serve God with every breath and heartbeat. Love serves. The religious life is a service of love — a lifelong loving service — or it is not the religious life. So the reflective aspirant, studying his Rule and Constitutions, comes to the realization that so long as he or she lives according to that Rule and those Constitutions, his or her entire life is spent exactly as God meant the lives of His rational beings to be spent; that every day, and every hour of the day and night, is filled to the full and, if possible, overflowing with glory for God. He knows with a knowledge that sets the whole being tingling, that the prime and ultimate purpose of his creaturehood is being fulfilled. That is very close to what is called beatitude.

This realization that what theologians call the *finis primarius creationis* — the first and final purpose of Creation — is being fulfilled right now, and will keep on being fulfilled so long as the fortunate individual lives within the Rule and according to the Constitutions, gives a peace of mind and tranquillity of soul that this world can neither give — nor take away. The religious who is sincere in his or her efforts to be all the religious calling demands knows the fullest satisfaction that a rational creature can know this side of the Beatific Vision. But that joy of the spirit does not mean that every day is gold with sunshine. It does not mean that there will not be personality clashes, human misunderstandings, misinterpretations of motives, and even belittling evaluations put on one's most honest efforts and genuine achievements. In other words, religious life is not lived in a world where roses are thornless, skies always cloudless, and gardens without a weed. In fact St. Benedict directs that all aspirants to his Order, be they males or females, be immediately made acquainted with the *dura et aspera* — those difficult and distasteful things: the austerities which human nature naturally shrinks from. But, come what may, the real religious, never loses that happiness of heart which comes from the knowledge that his every breath and heartbeat is God-directed, and pointed exactly as He wills.

The question immediately asserts itself: Is such a thing possible for a lay person? Can one who lives an entire life independently, without any immediate authority over him save that which governs Church and State in general, ever know the same surety about God's Will in his regard as does a religious? Can he come to similar peace of mind and know that same sense of fulfillment?

The only allowable answer to each and all of them is: He *must.* Yes, the lay person must come to do God's Will with every breath and heartbeat, or fail to be genuinely human, since he fails to be fully a rational creature.

The practical man may bridle at such statements and ask with some asperity: "How do I know it is God's Will that I be with this particular firm or company, that I be in this specific department, under this definite boss, and with this set of co-workers? How can I be sure that God wants me to be doing this one task, in this one place, at this precise moment?"

The answer to that barrage is: "Know yourself." For anyone who realizes that he is a creature, must immediately conclude that he would not and could not be what he is, where he is, with whom he is, doing what he is doing at this precise moment, did God will otherwise. That, of course, does not mean that God wills him to remain what he is, where he is, with whom he is, doing what he is doing for the rest of his days. No. But we are talking about the *now,* and we are saying it is filled with God's governance. Consequently there is absolutely nothing going on in this world of ours that God, in His providence, has not foreseen and foreordained. Therefore, everything, literally everything, that impinges in any way on every human being at this present moment has been willed by God — by a Will that is either directive or permissive. There are no accidents in God's world. There are only some happenings that have not been foreseen by humans; some occurrences that were not planned by man nor intended by him. But these, in the strictest sense of the word, are not accidents in God's world. They are happenings and occurrences which He knew from all eternity were going to take place *now.*

So the single persons of both genders can and must give every breath and heartbeat to God according to His Will. They may object and say they do not live in a married state or the religious state. But their objection vanishes when it is pointed out that they, like religious and the married, are creatures of God, redeemed by God's Son, conserved by the Father to be vivified by the Spirit, to make their specific contribution to that "re-establishing of all things in Christ." With the Triune God so interested in them, they should show similar interest in the Will of that Triune God. He wills that they, like the married and the religious, fulfill the duties of their own state — the state of creaturehood, which calls for a constant living in the state of grace, which is but another way of saying: living in Christ and having Christ living in them. That is the essence of human creaturehood; for that is the essence of Christianity.

But the Gospel's greatest lesson is not always learned — even by the most learned of Gospel commentators. That lesson can be summed up in one very telling word: *acceptance.*

Be careful of that word. It is tremendous. When used by a young maid in the tiny town of Nazareth it brought the Son of God, the Splendor of the Father's Glory, the only Eternal One, into time; it brought the omnipotent Creator into creaturehood; for as it fell from the lips of Mary Immaculate it inaugurated the re-creation of the human race by bringing God into flesh. She *accepted* God's Will for her, the role He had assigned her from all eternity. She did so by the simple word *Fiat.*

No human being would ever know anything like a sense of frustration if all would use that word as Mary did; if all would *accept* themselves as God made them; *accept* the one role He, in

His unfaltering wisdom and unfailing love, has assigned each; *accept* their place in the Mystical Body of Christ, and fulfill the one task that is theirs, and no one else's, in the universe.

Fiat — what a world of meaning in those two syllables. When spoken by a human it means that the individual human being will do all in his or her power to complete the Passion of Christ, turn redemption into salvation, and help God the Father "re-establish all things in Christ" — the Son.

Acceptance does not mean any mere nod of the head in agreement. No. It means that the human person stretches out eager hands to take from God whatever He wills to give, and to hug that gift to his heart. It means total dedication. It means love — the kind of love manifested by Christ who

> at his entrance into the world says,
> "Sacrifice and oblation you did not wish,
> but you have fitted together a body for me.
> You took no pleasure in burnt offerings
> and sin offerings.
> Then I said, 'Here I am; I have come
> to do your will, O God,'
> as it is written in the roll of the book!"
> (Hebr. 10:5–7)

It means that kind of love which lived in the Immaculate Heart of Mary when she said: "Regard me as the humble servant of the Lord. May all that you have said be fulfilled in me" (Lk. 1:38).

Acceptance, then, is something as tremendous as God, as love-filled as redemption, as efficacious, in its way, as the Cross of Christ. Ultimately, that is exactly what it means.

But now we must open our eyes as never before — and see just what is the Will of God for each individual human being. Again and again we have said it is to "re-establish all things in Christ." But we must yet ask what, in the concrete now, does that mean for this man and that woman. We have been insisting that it means that tremendous thing called *acceptance*. But the ordinary man and woman may yet look up in puzzlement and ask: "Accept what?"

The only answer is: *Christ!* Accept Him into your life and being. Let Him live the kind of life He wants to live in your living. Let

Him be your life: its length, its depth, its height, and breadth. Let Him be the principle and the end, not only of your every movement, but of the totality of all your movements. Let Him use your mind, your will, your emotions, your passions, every cell of your body, every faculty of your soul. Let Him have your every breath and heartbeat.

Not clear enough yet, is it? Not nearly concrete enough. Sounds more like rhetoric than reality. Yet, is not that a description of what Mary Immaculate accepted? Is that not something of a detailing of what Christ accepted when He said: "Here I am: I have come to do your will, O God"? Is not that itemizing exactly what we meant when at the threshold of the Sacrament of Baptism we were asked: "What do you seek?" and we replied: *"Faith."*

Whether we knew it or not, that word meant ever so much more than mere assent to the truths revealed to us by God; more than trust in God and His goodness; more than awe-filled and love-filled reverence for His being. That word meant even more than self-surrender. It meant, and it yet means, a personal, real, total, and a transforming relation to Jesus Christ. Genuine faith, in the sense of the New Testament, completely changes a human being. It effects that *metanoia* which was the first demand made by John the Baptist as he was fulfilling his role of Precursor to Christ; that *metanoia* which Christ claimed He had come to effect in sinners — and who is not of that number? — that *metanoia* Peter, in the first sermon preached by a vicegerent for Christ, commanded of his converts. It is conversion in the deepest, truest sense of that word; for it affects the whole man, changing his mind and heart, reversing all his values, orienting him to the true East which is beyond all earthly horizons. Faith, in the sense that is genuine, is renewal, rebirth, is the coming forth as a new creature — and all that newness streams from living in Christ and allowing Christ to live in us. That is vital faith. Nothing else is worthy of the Christian.

Baptism was rebirth; but like birth itself, it was only a beginning. Christ was born in us at that moment, and we were reborn in Christ. But from that moment to this present now — we have not really lived unless we have been growing and growing and growing in Christ — and He has been living as He desired in us. Life is action.

Human life is intellectual and volitional activity. Have we been thinking with the Mind of Christ? Have we been willing with His Will? That is why Christ was born of Mary. That is why God brought us into being. There precisely is the Will of God for each of us in the present moment.

What a simplification of life that can bring about. What security it can give to each of us who are so harried by insecurity. But do not think it works like some sort of magic. We must know how Christ's Mind and Will worked when He was on earth. We must know Christ. That calls for a prayerful study of the Gospels and the Acts, the Epistles and the Apocalypse. It calls for a prayerful, reflective reading of the Old Testament where Christ and His character are seen in type and prophecy. But, above all, it calls for frequent use of the sacraments — especially of the Holy Eucharist — and a conscious, continually living in the Sacrifice of the Mass. For it is only when we have been transformed into veritable hosts that we can dare to call ourselves Christians — and say we have done the Will of God.

St. Paul has said it all simply. Writing to the Galatians, he made it perfectly explicit when he declared: "It is no longer I that live, but Christ lives in me." It was an astounding statement and it called for explanation. Paul gave it in the next sentence when he wrote: "The physical life that I now live, I live by faith in the Son of God" (Gal. 2:20).

Now you can see why we dwelt on faith, and the *metanoia* it effects; why we have insisted that the whole lesson of the Gospel lies in the one word *acceptance;* why we have accented the fact that far from being passivity, that act of accepting God's Will for you in the now most often demands passion — love that knows no limit. Which is only another way of saying *Jesus Christ.*

The individual Christian who is sincere and serious about the Christian life may tell you he feels no different after baptism, confirmation, penance, and even after Holy Communion. But that does not mean that he is not different. Few of us have ever been conscious of our physical growth. We did not feel our arms and legs growing longer, our spinal column stretching out. Yet we grew. It is the same with Christ in us, and we in Christ. We will not feel our spiritual growth. We will not be conscious of our gradual transformation into Jesus. But if we are sincere Christians, serious about the Christian life, striving ever to know and do the Will of God in each succeeding now, that transformation will take place. Like all growth it will be gradual, imperceptible in the process, but real – and recognizable in effects.

To live with the life of God so that we can say as did St. Paul: "I live, now not I, but Christ lives in me," will not change anything in the externals of our earthly existence. The same *dura et aspera* that are found, not only in the Benedictine life, but in all human life, will appear for the Christian just as roughly and really as for the pagan. But the man in whom Christ lives, and who lives in Christ, will react interiorly quite differently to these *aspera et dura*." This fact must be dwelt upon; for too many seem to expect a miracle of some sort to take place once they strive to live their Christianity integrally and consciously.

The lawyer who endeavors to act as Christ would act were He a lawyer will find the law just as much of a labyrinth as it was before he made the effort to live in Christ and let Christ live in him. It will be just as difficult to draw up a brief, plead a case, or untangle a legal web. So, too with the surgeon and the medical man. The anatomy will be just as much of a marvel to the surgeon as before; and all his attention and skill will be required every moment of the operation. For the medical man diagnoses will be no whit less difficult, nor will prescriptions work with any greater surety or speed. And so for every other profession. Nothing changes in them – but there is a mighty change in those following the various professions. Each will go about his task with greater reverence, greater assurance that it is all worthwhile, greater interior peace. They will each be more conscious of the dignity that is theirs and more conscientious in living up to the obligations of that dignity. Because of Christ within them all things change, but most especially their estimation of passing things, and their appreciation of the value of the present moment.

The underwriters for insurance companies who labor to know and do the Will of God – and to do it in Christ and as Christ – will have to do everything an unbelieving underwriter does. The contact, the approach, the sales talk, the "breakdown" will all have to be made as made by the pagan underwriter. But there will be a difference — intangible, imponderable, but real and recognizable. There will be an aura about the Christ-conscious underwriter that will affect the very atmosphere surrounding the parties in the discussion. The prospect may think it simply the personality of the clever salesman, crediting the man with color and power that are anything but ordinary. But such an analysis is far too superficial. The Christ-bearer will lack many things the pagan possesses. The pressure exerted by each will be of an altogether different nature. From one it will be but glossed-over greed. From the other it will be something in the nature of that goodness which had a bent woman straighten up, a palsied man take up his bed and walk, and brought a dead brother back to his grieving sisters. The pagan may have sincerity, honesty, integrity, and a genuine concern for the welfare of his prospect. But the Christ-conscious man will have all that and more. What that more is, it is difficult to define. Christness, goodness, godliness sound exaggerated, yet they are quite exact; for it is grace that radiates out — and grace is a share in God who is Goodness.

But if the prospect is affected by the Christ-consciousness of the underwriter, the effects and affects in the underwriter himself are much greater. For him, selling insurance is a way of making a living — but it is much more besides: it it working with God for the temporal welfare of His children; it is doing the Will of our Father who is in heaven; it is fulfilling the purpose for which he was born — and much more so the purpose for which he was reborn. Such a man can meet success and failure in a way Rudyard Kipling never thought of when in his poem *If* he called those two "impostors" — and claimed that the real man treats success and failure "just the same." The Christ-conscious man does not call them "impostors"; he recognizes them for what they are: messengers from God as real as was Gabriel when he appeared in Nazareth. He knows they bear much the same message; for he knows our Father's plan to "re-establish all things in Christ." Hence, for him, every event in his life is but a "coming of Christ" who is asking him to carry on His Incarnation. Now it will be with the success Christ knew when

He first began to preach; now again with the surprising and supreme failure that Christ knew at the end. But whatever God wants, this man wants; hence, so long as he is conscious of having done his utmost, he accepts the results as God's Will for him — and says: "Thank you" with as much sincerity after failure as after success. For such a man life is ever so much more than making a living, even while making a living is crammed to the full, and even overflowing with the life of God.

There is a serenity about this man well worth analysis. It is not merely that control every human being worthy of the name should labor for and acquire; nor is it simply that calm which is more than mastery of facial features and our ever expressive arms, hands, and fingers. This man has more to him and more about him than that air of dignity and even of majesty which surrounds those who are in command of their interior self, who have their emotions and passions well controlled. The tranquillity which this man carries about with him and to some extent causes in others by his mere presence is not the result of temperament but the inevitable effect of his vital possession of a vital truth. This man is serene. This man is benign. This man is not only sympathetic, understanding, kind, gentle, and generous; he is thoroughly and even contagiously human simply because he has become completely convinced and, consequently, continually conscious that God is his Father who is ever provident. Hence, he must act as befits a child of God. There is only one way for such a person to act — and that is with warm love.

Whenever you come in contact with such a person, you are struck by two things: his serenity and his joy. Both bubble up and flow out from the one truth of his faith: *God is his Father,* who is Love. The child of God then labors to incarnate that axiom which runs: "Like Father, like son."

It is the vivid humanness of the individual that impresses you first. But then you slowly become aware of the fact that there is an added luster to his human personality, a quality to his down-to-earth appreciation of things, that lifts him above the earth and somehow above the ordinary human. Now you are at the heart of the matter; for now you see that God's Will for the ordinary man is that he be thoroughly human, but with a thoroughness only those humans achieve who live in Christ, the perfect Human, and allow Christ, the Divine, to live in them. It is that which we call by the beautiful name of grace, a name which should speak to us of God and His sharing of divine life with us humans, which explains all that we have been analyzing in this God-conscious man who labors to do the Will of God always. It is this share in God's life that explains this man's living; that gives him his serenity, benignity, joy, and love. He knows that God is breathing every breath with him and in him. Why should he be other than serene — even as worlds shatter? Why should he be other than joy-filled — even as his heart breaks with sorrow and his whole body and soul are filled with pain? Faith has effected a *metanoia; metanoia* has re-evaluated everything on earth; this re-evaluation has him saying *Fiat* to everything; for he accepts everything as part of God's plan for him *in Christ.* His joy is the joy of the saints. His life is a life of real love.

Such a man truly senses, in as far as he can, truth. The sights, the sounds, the smells, the solidity or nonsolidity of things they bring to this man's consciousness come to him as "sacred signs." Each speaks to him of his Father, telling him of that Love which has prepared a whole world of loveliness just for him. Each insists that it is to be used with reverence and relish. He knows that it is God's Will for him that he find Jesus Christ all about him. In all truth he leads a sacramental life: the visible things of this world lead him on to the *invisibilia Dei* — the Goodness, the Love that is God. He accepts God in rose, rain and rainbow, in storm as well as in sun, in sickness just as much as — if not more than! — in radiant health. The fact is that this man has not only accepted things as from God, he has accepted God in the things themselves, and accepted in such a way as to assimilate God in himself. The word is not too strong, even though it startles our weak piety and shocks our weak faith. Christ told us that if we did not eat His flesh and drink His blood we would not have life in us. But food and drink never sustained life in anyone. It is only the food and drink that is assimilated. So also with this divine Food — not only of Holy Communion, but of all the holiness in everything with which mortals may commune — and that takes in all nature.

If we not only receive Christ in everyone and everything, but actually assimilate Him after the reception, then we will express Him in all that we do and in all that we are. Such is the law of life or, in better words, the Will of God.

What has been said about Christ beating in the blood of an insurance salesman and breathing in his every breath can be said of any other man in any other profession or employment so long as he knows and does the Will of God. But perhaps too much has been said about the "ordinary man" and not nearly enough about the "ordinary woman."

There is no difficulty in discovering the Will of God for the ordinary woman who is wife and mother. She has only one duty — to love. She has only one destiny — to become her real self. A wife and a mother can never be small, mean, selfish — and claim the sacred names of wife and mother. She must ever be what Mary was and Christ is: love that is sacrifice — and sacrifice that is love. The Will of God for her is something so sublime that the best in art centers around her God-given vocation. And let it be said with finality that this vocation is God-given and is the usual vocation for women. Only blindness to the obvious in nature and deafness to the clarity of Revelation could ever question this fact. God has made woman physically and psychologically different from man; shaping her body and soul for a particular purpose: that of being the companion to man and the mother of men. The two, in reality, are but different aspects or applications of the one thing: maternity. A good wife actually "mothers" her husband by so participating in his life that she brings to birth the deepest and best that is in him. Companionship, on this level, is life-giving. Thus husband and wife become one in every way possible, and always with a vital result. The Will of God is manifest in what is called the "psychology of women." They are interested in the living, the personal, the concrete; they are inclined to obedience, service, and sacrifice; they long for that complete self-surrender which is the heart and soul of love. That is how God made them. Their duty is *to be themselves* as God made them. That, of course, calls for a *metanoia;* for they, too, have inherited a tainted nature. That is why their innate tendency to the personal too often begins and ends in their own person; why their attraction to the concrete becomes curiosity, and their tendency to give themselves to others makes them altogether too possessive and even plain busybodies. So to become what she is, every woman needs the grace of God; she needs that acceptance shown by that woman of all women who said *Fiat*. But no woman will ever say that with the magnanimity of which each is capable unless she has a faith that is living and filling her life with a keen consciousness of the closeness of God and the all-pervasiveness of His ever loving providence.

The woman who taught them their most expressive word is the woman who shows them the way to life and the way to love. Mary Immaculate centered her life in her Child — who was also her God. She accepted God's Will at the Annunciation and did it right through to her own Assumption. Her questioning of Gabriel shows what a *metanoia* she had to undergo. Her answer to the same angel tells all women the kind of *metanoia* they must undergo. It must be total: not only God-centered, but God-circumferenced and completely saturated with God. The lesson of all lessons for wives and mothers to learn from Mary is that they, like her, are to do not what they like but only what God desires. See how Mary accepted God's desire regarding Joseph and his concern over her obvious pregnancy. See how she accepted God's desire about the place her Child should be born. See how she sacrificed home and homeland for the sake of that Child's life. See how she brought Him up in the seclusion of Nazareth. Totally dedicated, completely committed to the Father's Will for His, and her, Son, she was truly God's handmaid; for she had no will of her own save that of doing His Will. This Child was but a Trust she had from God, a Gift that was to be given back, a Talent incarnate that was to be more than doubled. In Mary, every woman can see and recognize the fundamental attitude of soul that is alone proper; for it is the only one that corresponds fully to woman's vocation: helpmate to man because handmaid of God. As wife and mother she was selfless and thus both manifested and developed her true selfhood. Her devotion to Joseph and Jesus was devotion to God. She fulfilled herself by emptying herself, pouring out all she had and was in her quiet, consistent, persistent concentration on being what God wanted her to be: just Mary of

Nazareth, wife of the village carpenter and mother of Jesus, the carpenter's Son. This glamorless girl was God's choice for Queen of the universe, a position she won by the simple expedient of being what she was called to be, and doing what she was asked to do. Mary is the vivid proof that real success in life is assured to all who will be sincere enough to adopt the simple expedient of doing their duty; that a woman's way to love, which is her only real life, is wide open: all she need do is listen to the message each new "Gabriel" brings her, and say "Yes" to God.

In the present state of society many a young girl will be visited by a "Gabriel" whose message will contain the same request from God, but will be expressed in almost opposite words. She will be asked to give Christ the place in her life and being that He had in Mary's; she will be asked to "incarnate" the Word of God without ever becoming a wife and mother. Hers will be the vocation of bringing Christ to birth, of saving His life from other Herods, of helping Him "advance in age, wisdom and grace before God and man," of being with him at other Canas, and on other Calvarys — as she follows what is called a "career."

Of course there is only one career for any human being — that of doing the Will of the Father. But the Father's Will, which is Himself, is of infinite variety. Hence, not every woman is called by God to be wife and mother, or even simply wife. There is a divine vocation for some women to be career women, in the professions, in trade, and in industry — and even in the home. Fatherless children may need a breadwinner. Orphaned brothers and sisters may need one to mother them. Aged parents may need to be supported. Overburdened mothers and fathers may need assistance. God's Will is manifest for the girls who find themselves facing these needs which they alone can fill. "Gabriel" is before them awaiting their *Fiat.* They can conceive and bring forth Christ truly — else Incarnate Truth lied; for He one day said: "Anyone that does the will of God is brother or sister or mother to me" (Mk. 3:35).

But even outside the home and in the professional and business world, single women can, and do, have vocations from God. For, first of all, there is no profession that has not been practiced — and successfully so — by women. There are today women doctors, women lawyers, women educators. Aside from the one exception of becoming ordained priests in the Catholic Church, women can function in every other profession. Some, of course, are more natural to her: nursing, teaching, social service. In these those distinctly feminine characteristics, which are maternal, will find scope. Obviously, then, it is the Will of God that they exercise these characteristics in such fields.

Perhaps single women working — say in a publishing house — will have wondered if they have been doing the Will of God, if God could have given them a "vocation" to such a way of life. The questioning, of course, is a sign of doubt and insecurity. Consequently they feel frustrated.

That should never be. What these women need is *acceptation*. They have to accept the fact that God has not destined every individual female to become wife and mother; to accept the fact that it was God, the Infinitely Wise One, who made them as they are physically and psychologically — and God never makes a mistake; to accept the fact that every ability they have in the intellectual, emotional, social line is a talent entrusted to them by God with which they are to "trade until He comes." Once they accept these realities, they will see that their vocation is just as religious, in its way, as is that which is called a religious vocation; for each comes from God and each is for God. Then they will be led on to the further realization that they, in their single state, further God's plan just as effectively as do wives, mothers, and nuns. For it is as much a part of God's universal plan that there be publishing houses as it is that there be homes and convents, even though there is a great difference in them.

What has been said of publishing houses is true of any other trade. Edith Stein, the German Jewish philosopher, who was converted to Catholicism, then became a Carmelite nun, only to be hunted down by the Gestapo and sent to her death by Hitler in the gas chambers of Auschwitz, and who wrote and lectured much on "The Vocation of Man and Woman According to Nature and to Grace," said: "the call of God, which can be made as clear by external circumstances as by inclination of the heart, should be accepted neither rebelliously nor resignedly, but with willing cooperation." What a prescription for peace of mind, joy of heart, and thrill in living! In her quiet philosophical way she went on to surmise that "if the call to the virginal life is received with joy, even though it may not include the religious state nor be in accordance with natural inclinations, there will be strong probability that the feminine nature will not suffer harm." She could have gone further. She could have safely promised that the feminine nature would gain by such a joyous acceptation. For it was she who in another lecture said that "the deepest desire of a woman's heart is to surrender itself lovingly to another, to be wholly his and to possess him wholly," then went on to point out that "only God can receive the complete surrender of a person, and in such a way that she will not lose, but gain her soul. And only God can give Himself to a human being in such a way that He will fulfill its whole being. . . . Hence, the total surrender, which is the principle of the religious life, is at the same time the only possible adequate fulfillment of woman's desires."

This brilliant Jewess convert immediately pointed out that that did not mean that every woman must become a nun if she would fulfill her nature and answer her vocation. But it does mean that no woman will ever be herself as God wills her to be unless she is totally surrendered to God. Where or how that surrender takes place: in the home, in the public limelight, in the deep cloister of a convent, makes no difference. The truth is that each woman everywhere must have the mind and heart of that Maid of Nazareth who said: "May all that you have said be fulfilled in me"; for each and every woman has been called into being just to become an *ancilla Domini* — "a humble servant of the Lord."

So every breath and heartbeat of a woman editor, advertising manager, proofreader, stenographer; every heartbeat and breath of a physical therapist, laboratory technician, nurse, or nurse's aide; every breath and heartbeat of every woman in every walk of life belongs to God. It is His Will that they be given to Him as each comes along in every new moment.

We are back to the basic plan and original as well as ultimate vocation for every human: to be Christ's mystical member, living with His life, and allowing Him to live on in our lives. That vocation demands every breath and heartbeat. It is the Will of God that they be given in Christ and as Christ. No woman will ever equal the tenderness of Jesus; nor will any man come near His strength. So Christ is Model for both – His grace alone can help each to bring nature to perfection and set both man and woman standing before their worlds radiating the realities God wills them to: His mastery over creation as they protect and preserve every creature given to their care, and His powerful paternity as they bring forth and bring up children for His Kingdom by spiritual as well as physical motherhood and fatherhood.

God's Will is clear enough for one who wants to think. Each of us was made to manifest God, to mirror forth His goodness, to pulse with His praise. There is the necessity, of course, for reflection on this fundamental truth and for a vital realization of God's plan and purpose for each of us every split second of our existence. Such reflection is really mental prayer. Its fruit will be that vital life-giving and life-forming conviction that Christ in us and we in Christ is the only answer to any and every question. Once we have garnered this fruit, our *metanoia* is accomplished – and we live. Our lives take on a new seriousness which is most always shown in a fresher joyousness. We are ever so much more sure of ourselves; certain about what is right and what is wrong; free from every fear but the fear of losing Christ; dynamic and purposeful without the slightest trace of drives or of being driven – save perhaps to those discerning ones who will see we are *caritate Christi compulsi* – spurred on by the love of Christ for all who should be in Christ. We will be found men and women who need no psychiatrist to calm our fears, dissipate our anxieties, free us from compulsions, and build up our egos. We will be integrated personalities who never need run to the druggist for "happiness pills" or tranquilizers. For we will have found our all in Christ Jesus, and be able to give our all to life and love by being His members.

Some may say this is an oversimplification for our complicated world and its mode of existence. They may insist upon the effects environment has on everyone. But we may as well stop them there and tell them it is time that they decide to affect their environment more than their environment affects them. God's Will is that we be lords of the universe about us — not its slaves. Hilda Graef saw the solution and gave it to the public in an essay entitled *No Time to Pray.** She knows it is God's Will that we "pray always." She also knows that we have a civilization geared to anything and everything but prayer.

Hilda Graef saw the difficulty and the solution: "bring God into all our activities." She even sensed the truth that every breath and heartbeat is to bear on God's Will; for she wrote:

> Perhaps it might be a help to think deliberately for a few moments that the work I am going to do is the will of God for me since it is to contribute to my own and my family's livelihood; that the recreation I am about to take is also God's Will for me, since relaxation is necessary for man to keep up his capacity for work. In fact, a kind of grace before work and recreation may be as beneficial and sanctifying as grace before meals. In such a way it would be possible to refer all the activities of our day to God without having to recite long prayers.

This German convert almost arrived at the conclusion reached by the French Catholic, François Mauriac, who in his *Secret of the Saints* said: "prayer is taking a direction; it is pointing everything to God." Miss Graef finally concluded that "what we need is the full integration of prayer into our life, into the rhythm of work and recreation, so that we do not feel it as something alien, but as one of the elements of our day, indeed as the source from which we draw our strength, the hub of our existence."

This woman knows God has made His Will explicit through St. Paul when He had this Jewish convert tell his pagan converts that they were to "pray without ceasing." Miss Graef knows that God does not will the impossible nor do His directives become ineffectual because of changes in times and conditions of peoples. She realizes they must be fulfilled today just as really as in Paul's day — the ways of fulfillment alone will differ. Nothing can keep a man or woman from giving all they have, and are, and do to God. For this donation is a free-will offering, and no one on earth, nor anyone from hell, can touch the free will of any man or woman. It is all a matter of prayer — but prayer in the true sense of the word.

* In *Cross and Crown,* December, 1959.

To say prayers is the last meaning of the verb *to pray* — and one may dare say it is the least meaning. Mauriac is right: prayer is taking a direction or, better, giving direction not only to all we do, think, say — but to all we are. Prayer is a state of being. Prayer is a life. For the Christian, prayer is *living in Christ* and learning from the *Spirit of Christ* to do hour after hour, *now* after *now,* what will please *the Father.* We are not on earth to learn how to say prayers — but how to become and to be a prayer. Everything that we do, everything that we are is to be praise, gratitude, reparation, adoration, and supplication. It was for Christ; it is to be for every real Christian.

The woman, called by God, to live alone and follow a career, wakes in the morning to a new *now.* That very waking is to be a prayer, made so by her will which turns that awakening to God who gives it to her. She bathes, dresses, breakfasts — all can be, and should be, prayer: conscious conformity to God's Will for her right now. If she has time and she is wise, she goes to assist in Christ's Sacrifice, and receives Christ in Communion. What a shame it is that there are so few "wise virgins" in our world! These life-giving, love-filled Gifts of God: Holy Mass and Holy Communion, with "oil" enough in them to fill not only the lamps of the virgins, but the whole lives of the virgins, and set them shining with the very splendor of God in this dark world of ours, are left almost as was the oil of the "foolish virgins" in that fear-provoking parable! But if our career woman is not wise enough to go to Holy Communion actually, she must be smart enough to make a spiritual Communion before, or during, or at least after her breakfast, so that she can set off for work with Christ pulsing in her veins and she alert to His throbbing there. Once at work, she radiates Christ in her own feminine fashion, bringing to the fore all the wonderful attributes God has so lavishly given to the female species. It is God's Will that women help civilize man. She will fulfill that Will of God only by remaining what she is: the gentler of the sex, the more refined, the more selfless, sacrificial, and sacramental. May one not say the more holy?

This "wise virgin" must remember not only what she is, namely, a female, but even more acutely, who she is: Christ. She is His member. She lives with His life. She is to spread about that "fragrance of Christ" Paul spoke of in his Epistle to the Corinthians. "We are the fragrance of Christ for God," he said, just after he had pointed out that God always leads us "in Christ, and spreads about his knowledge like a perfume everywhere through our instrumentality" (2 Cor. 2:14, 15). That is this girl's calling. That is the calling of every Christian. It is so awesome a calling that Paul himself asked: "Who is competent to perform such a task?" The answer to that question is: everyone who in Christ and as Christ becomes what God wills every human to become: an ever breathing adoration.

This girl we are using as model has made her morning uninterrupted prayer, praise, and pleasure for God by making it uninterrupted obedience to His Will. She will do the same with lunch hour and her afternoon of labor. Dinner may come after a cocktail party and be prelude to a ball. Every *now* in these hours of recreation, relaxation, and relish of social life can be, and should be, prayer, praise, and pleasure for God. They will be if this virgin is wise enough to take them as His Will for her and directs them to Him who gives them.

Christ was at banquets and the equivalent of balls. Christ was at a wedding feast. Christ socialized, fraternized, relaxed at Bethany with Martha, Mary, and Lazarus. So there is no realm in which the Christian is without a Model. Christ very truly was "as we *in all things*, sin alone excepted." A fact which gives relevance and even a personal pertinence to the passage in Paul's letter to the Thessalonians which set Hilda Graef wondering if we moderns had time enough to pray. "Always be joyful," says Paul. "Never cease praying. Always be grateful. Such sentiments God wills you to have in Christ Jesus. Do not extinguish the Spirit. Do not despise the utterances he inspires, yet test them all. Hold on to that which is good, and have nothing to do with any kind of evil" (1 Thess. 5:16–22).

There is God's Will for this girl we have in mind, expressed by Himself through St. Paul. The wondrous fact is that God has entrusted Himself to each of us in Christ Jesus. This Incarnate Word of God, and very God Himself, did not come to us only as the Babe of Bethlehem or the Crucified Man of Calvary. He comes to us now — and not only in Revelation or through His living representatives: the pope, prelates, and priests, but He comes to each of us personally and in Person. And it is His Will that we be responsible for God every second that we live. We have accepted God in baptism. It is our delightful duty to keep God living within us and to keep ourselves alive in God. So if this girl we have been talking about is employed by nonbelievers, what a vocation is hers! God wills that she reveal Him to those who as yet know Him not. She will do so by remaining what God made her — a woman with all those feminine traits that make her different from man; and a Christian woman who, like Jesus, "goes about doing good."

Often there is no great difficulty in knowing God's Will for any of us from this second to the next and on to the last. There may be a moment's hesitancy when we have several possibilities before us, each equally good, as far as we can see in the light of Christ. Then we are to choose that one which appeals to us most; for the very appeal comes from God and can be taken as manifestation of His Will in our regard. If each holds an equal appeal we can be sure we will be doing God's Will no matter which we choose. The main thing in life is to have our wills screwed to the determination of "seeking first the kingdom of God and his justice"; this will be actual only if we are God-conscious and Christ-conscious individuals. That is the essence and quintessence of human living since a young girl sent an archangel back to heaven with the word *Fiat* as answer to God.

But man must be truly realistic before he can grasp this reality. It is not apprehended by imagination — like a fairy tale or some parable. It is not grasped by mere observation and the unaided powers of the intellect. It is taken in only by faith — a strong faith, a living, open-eyed, generous faith. For the world about us seems to be shouting "Lie!" to all we believe about God and His providence. Hence, we have to open our eyes to Reality. We have to open our hearts and lovingly accept Reality. We have to stir up memory and have us greet Reality as Mary did at Nazareth, the Magi at Bethlehem, the Baptist by the Jordan, Peter at Caesarea-

Philippi, Dismas on Calvary, Thomas in the Upper Room on the Octave of Easter. We must believe and, consequently *know* that "every event is a coming of Christ" and that we are to give every breath and heartbeat to God.

When any man becomes what God wills him to become, things fall in place — all things, even, and especially the hardest — and God's pattern is slowly discerned. We sense behind, and even in, the forces that seem to shape and govern events Something and Someone else: the omnipotence of God and our Father. Then we can believe Paul when he says: "Now we know that God causes all things to work together for the good of those who love him" (Rom. 8:28). The conviction forms — it deepens and becomes ever more alive — that we are part of God's plan, that we are here and now helping Him run His world and "re-establish all things in Christ." The truth pulses in our body and all our being that we are His members with a work to do: we are to "fill up what is wanting . . . for His Church."

To be a Christian means to live with the life of Christ — and to live the entire Christ-life. That will mean both Gethsemani and Golgotha. But these are only means to Easter's empty tomb, the ascent from Mount Olivet, and the enthronement at the right of the Father. Such is God's Will for every man and every woman. Dante was right: "In His Will is our peace." We will have peace only when we live the life of Christ through to the end. It is the whole that brings peace; the peace Christ promised when He said: "Peace is my legacy to you: my own peace is my gift to you. My giving to you is not like the world's way of giving" (Jn. 14:27).

That is what we are to remember now and always: His giving is not like the world's way of giving. His giving often looks like taking. Romano Guardini has said that "every Christian one day reaches the point where he must be ready to accompany the Master into destruction and oblivion: into that which the world considers folly, that which for his own understanding is incomprehensible, for his own feeling intolerable. Whatever it be: suffering, dishonor, the loss of loved ones or the shattering of a lifetime's work, this is the decisive test of his Christianity." You see why. Because it is a test whether he really believes in God or not; whether he actually realizes that he is Christ, and that it is God's Will *now* to "re-establish all things in Christ" through him.

To show that it is possible to be Christ and give every breath and heartbeat to God; to realize that there are Christians today who "accompany the Master into destruction" let us meet some peace-filled Christs who are modern Americans. In them we will see Guardini's promise and prophecy fulfilled. He said: "One way or another we must brush the depths Christ divinely plummeted, taste the dregs he drained to the last drop. . . . From this unreserved realization of the Father's will comes the illimitable peace of Christ, also for us."

CHAPTER TEN

IT CAN BE DONE . . . NOW

It has been said often enough, but it has too seldom been believed: There is only one real evil in the world: sin. Why is it that so few accept that truth? Can it be because they see, feel, taste, touch, and hear evil all day long without ever realizing that what they so readily call and know to be evil is really sin? Atheistic communism is evil — very evil. And the practice of atheistic communism is sin. The A-bomb and the H-bomb and all other such bombs can be evil; for the A-, H-, and every other bomb can be sin. *Laissez-faire* capitalism was evil. The practice of *laissez-faire* capitalism was sin. Racial segregation is evil. Racial segregation is sin.

These truths must be told; for it is all too obvious that we are losing our sense of sin.

But even more obvious is the fact that we are losing our sense of reality, so these other truths must be told. Cancer is not sin. Therefore cancer is not evil. Heart trouble is not sin. Therefore heart trouble is not evil. Financial failure is not sin. Therefore financial failure is not evil. Disease, disability, death itself are not sins. Therefore they are not evils. Each can be, the last most certainly will be, God's Will for me at any moment. How will I meet them?

It is tragic, but it is true, that our day is afraid of only two things: the H–Bomb — and the Spirit of Christ. Could our world be freed from its fear of Christ and His Spirit, the first fear would vanish of itself — as would every other groundless fear, especially that foolish fear of sickness, suffering, and death.

At the base of the Rocky Mountains there is a family of seven girls and two young boys whose father was struck with polio eight years ago and has hardly lived outside an iron lung since. He was not a wealthy man before he was struck. His wife claims to be the mother of the "most popular paupers in the country." They call their home "Maryland," not only because each girl bears Mary's name, but because they are conscious that, not only the father of the family, but the mother and every member has a vocation from God; that they, like Mary, are to allow God the Holy Spirit form Christ in them. They are conscious, too, that while there will always be suffering in Mary's land, there never will be any sin — hence, there will be no evil; consequently, they are always bubbling over with joy! This is a *Christian* family — out there at the base of the Rockies. They know that there is more than one Holy Land on earth; that not only that bit of territory washed by the Jordan River, but that every bit of territory washed by any river is meant by the Will of God to be a land filled with holiness. They see the Rockies as the Rockies, but they also recognize them as very like Mount Olivet. At the base of that mountain Christ agonized. From the summit of that mountain Christ, after His agony and death, ascended. At the base of any and every mountain Christians may agonize. If they do so in Christ Jesus and as Jesus Christ, they will know something very like His Ascension after they have gone through their passion and death.

That is something of the vision shared by this family of twelve. They believe. That is the whole story. They believe that by baptism they were made members of Christ. From that fact, everything else follows logically — and gloriously. This family radiates joy. That will puzzle only the pagan and the pagan-minded. Who would not be filled to overflowing with joy who once realized that he or she had been chosen by God to function as Christ and thus "fill up what is wanting." Here is what the wife and mother wrote in a letter to me:

> On October 2, 1952, the feast of St. John Leonard, my good husband, John Leonard, was stricken with spinal bulbar polio, and has been paralyzed from the neck down ever since. I am sure there are no mere coincidences in the plans of Providence! Our eldest daughter was then eleven, and our second son and baby, "Beppo" was born five months after John was in the iron lung. At that time

they performed a second tracheotomy. The doctors said he could live only twenty minutes. Today, seven years later, he is still alive, still totally paralyzed, and I am sure has done a greater job for our dear Lord in his silent apostolate of suffering than if he had been the tremendous success he seemed destined to be in the business world at the time he was stricken. John is now forty-eight years old and has been an inspiration to all who have visited him, proof positive that if we accept God's Will He will sustain us solely on divine strength until our job or mission in His plan of Redemption is completed. . . . God has His finger on John's pulse, and, actually I don't think we have ever had more security before in all our lives. . . . How few people in life face up to their cross and realize it is really their crown for all eternity.

A little over a year later this same woman wrote:

John is still with us, *Deo gratias!* This is only about the tenth time that all the doctors have been *so* definite about their prognoses — and so wrong! God's providence continues to surround us on all sides. . . . The morning the doctors delivered their verdict, nine of the nursing nuns from St. Jo's came over to bid John farewell. They have told me since that not one of them expected him to live through that day. But, manalive, as you are wont to say, he is still a man alive, pulsing with God's love and suffering constantly, except when sleeping under very heavy sedation — and I have yet to hear his first complaint! How pleasing to our dear Lord must be his silent apostolate and incomparable resignation. Pray on, Father, that God's Will be fully accomplished in him — and that I may add whatever support He expects of me.

Holy Saturday night your dear little Mary Agnes popped the question to her dad: Could she enter the convent come fall? — Then she turned and asked if *I* would rather she stay around a while and help me educate the young 'uns. Lord of the Living! I told her *I* need her as much as I need a hole in the head. The whippersnapper! to think that after eight years of proof positive, she would doubt the Lord's providence for us.

"The Whippersnapper" herself wrote:

Mom and Dad were overwhelmed when I asked them (for nobody, including yours truly, ever expected it!). And they were utterly overjoyed. Daddy has already made my whole religious life worthwhile by revealing: "There have been many selfish elements in my Cross, Mary A., one of the deepest was an intense desire to see the fruition of my suffering before going Home. You gave me more than I expected with this decision. Now I can truly say: "Any time, Lord!" . . . Imagine *me* being able to give Him something as dear to His heart as that. *Domine, non sum dignus. . . .*

The same Mary Agnes used to greet her father on October 2 each succeeding year with a poem for the anniversary of the manifestation of God's Will for him in that precious *now.* The year she decided God's Will for her was that she enter the convent, her father had suffered another of those "last moments." She wrote for that anniversary:

Angel of Death,
Delay thy heavy hand –
These ageing, fungused, purple lips
Would speak:

My God,
Forgive my past and hear
The final wish your suffering son
Would plead.

This, from my life,
Let Justice but recall:
Not what I may have done these years,
But *why!*

My precious cross
To His has been compared –
What Joy: that I was made to mirror
Him!

I beg
In Judgement's moments tense,
Stress effort, love – not just effects
I've made.

My Mass –
A life spent nailed to Love:
This lesson's worth is all I've tried
To teach

I was Your lamp.
'Tis You, I pray, shone forth!
In memory, more, I seek not me,
But You! !

My legacy
To my nine precious souls:
The key to life: *Your Love to love* –
Even black pain.

But how these lips
Can leave and thank my wife?
As selfless, dear as His Mary
To Him!

I ache to try –
But blended souls can't part.
My presence leaves; my heart
In hers shall stay.

To pay my debt –
A promise that I'll save
Eternity's best joys to share
With her.

The Angel comes,
Her white hand nears my brow –
My dying plea to those I leave:
Live Love! !

To Love I go;
My soul in trembling peace
Ascends. The drama ends. God, I
Come Home!

What, my reward?
I ask: Paralysis –
Again, and always, let me lie
In utter, helpless proof of love
Beneath Your Feet!*

Among those who believe passionately this is typical rather than exceptional. What other explanation is possible of Mary Ellen Kelly who charmed the world with her autobiography: *But With the Dawn, Rejoicing?* This young Iowan realized that it was God's Will for her that she be fixed to a bed for all her days, with ability to move only her eyes, and her hand the space of a short word. She knew she had a vocation. That it was just like Christ's. She must "do His Will." She also knew that, unlike Christ, she could, in

* (Published here for the first time, with permission of the Author.)

her own words, be a "flop" at it. So what did she do? Seized on the truth that she, in every passing *now,* has all the time there is in the world, and has only one thing to do with it: His Will. She does it by sanctifying every second. In fact that is the title she gives to the sheet she edits for shut-ins whom she has organized into a world-wide Sodality of Mary. Again we find ourselves in "Maryland" as we contact people who know the only evil in the world is sin, and that suffering is most frequently God's greatest blessing.

These people know what it is to be a *"dispensator mysteriorum Dei"* as Paul told his Corinthians he was. "We are stewards of God's mysteries," he wrote, then added: "what in final analysis is required of stewards is that they prove to be trustworthy" (1 Cor. 4:1, 2). Just prior to this he had said: "We are God's co-workers" (1 Cor. 3:9) or as one has wisely translated it: "God's helpers." That is the truth that gives zest to such a vocation as that enjoyed by Mary Ellen Kelly and John Leonard. These souls realize the truth of what Pascal himself perhaps never fully realized when he wrote: "Think what you will, but you will never approach happiness without approaching its source, which is God and Christ."

Blindness is not a sin, but how many would consider it a blessing? So much of our life and real living depends on sight! Yet there is one American woman of radiant joy who lost her sight when only two months old. In the summer of 1888 a doctor, while examining little Genevieve Caulfield, knocked over a bottle of medicine as she herself puts it: "with his elbow; the caustic fluid splashed all over my face and into my upturned eyes." From that day to this Genevieve Caulfield has never seen. But she has lived a full life — and a very exciting one. Traveling to Japan, she proved that the blind can make their own way in the world of the sighted; from there she went to Bangkok, where she established a school for the blind, and silenced all those who had been saying "the blind are incapable of learning." At present, in her seventy-second year, she is busy in Vietnam, starting another school and helping to set up a national program for the blind. The secret of it all is told in her book *The Kingdom Within.** That "kingdom," of course, is the King-

* Harper, 1960.

dom of God, as Christ once told the Pharisees who were asking "When is the Kingdom of God coming?" (Lk. 17:20.)

"My heart is full," she writes in the final paragraph of her book, "as I contemplate the Kingdom within us all makes it possible for us, despite the worst apparent handicaps, to do the work of God on earth. When I was talking about this book to a friend in America, he suggested, 'Bring the story to a dramatic climax.' But I don't know how I can. The story and I can only go on and on; for that is what life is, the process of going on and on until the work for which we were created comes to an end."

How perfectly this blind woman has learned the meaning and the purpose of our life on earth: to "go on and on" which can only mean living from moment to moment – doing God's Will. For that is precisely what she means by completing the work for which we were created. This indomitable woman knows that a life's work is done only in a life's time.

Helen Keller may have taught more than one of us a lesson. But it waited for Genevieve Caulfield to show us how unselfish a woman can be, how belief in God can give one courage enough to take one of nature's greatest liabilities and turn it into a very real asset. Miss Caulfield knows there are no accidents with God, and that in this world sin is the only evil. She knows now why God allowed that doctor to be so clumsy back in 1888; for had he not tipped over that bottle which burned out her sight she would never have got to Japan, Thailand, or Vietnam as easily as she did, nor do one-hundredth part of the work she has already accomplished. She is one who can now say with St. Paul, "Indeed, all things work together unto good for those who love Him" (Rom. 8:28). Her life teaches with that eloquence born only of action that God's providence is personal and that if we walk with Him all we need is a will to trust and love: eyes do not matter, hands are not absolutely necessary, we can walk into heaven without feet; we can serve God and man in blindness, deafness, speechlessness, and even in total paralysis provided we believe and love.

The phrase is hackneyed, but the truth it tells is anything but hackneyed: "Blessings" do come in disguise. Genevieve Caulfield proves that — as does Clare Boothe Luce. When the Jesuit priest who wrote her so steadily after the tragic death of her beloved daughter, kept telling her that "it was a blessing in disguise," Clare, with some asperity, replied that "if it were, then the disguise was perfect." She did not see it then; for she had not yet come to the realization that there is only one real evil in the world — and that is not death. She knows now. She also knows how loving is our God.

People who believe and think can always pierce disguises. I have in mind a young lawyer in the Midwest who as a result of trouble with his wife took to drink, then to dope. These two caused more trouble with the wife. And so he went in this truly vicious circle until he met a girl who openly confesses she was both an alcoholic and a drug addict. She broke the lawyer's vicious circle by pointing out to him the simplicity of life when one believes and thinks, then acts on that belief and thought. She went so far as to say that God wanted her to become both an alcoholic and a drug addict just that she might help every alcoholic and addict she meets. She is wrong, of course, in the way she phrases it. God never wanted her to become either a drunkard or an addict. He permitted her to use — or rather, to abuse — her free will. He permitted her to become what she wanted to become at that time. But all the while He had but one will for her — that she be converted and live; that she undergo a *metanoia* and find love; that she at last surrender to Him. Now she sees through the disguise of sin — and recognizes the world's only evil. Now also she sees that "all things — even such a lapse as was hers — work together unto good for those who love God" (Rom. 8:28). Now she stands forth as an embodiment, as it were, of that ever necessary distinction between God's so-called "permissive Will" — which is no will at all — and God's real Will. Like Magdalen and Augustine, like many another son of Adam and daughter of Eve, this woman realizes that "what God wills is your sanctification" (1 Thess. 4:3) and because He permitted her to fall and fall, she must love Him all the more; and show that love by doing His Will with joy.

People like these, who have been picked up by God from shattering falls, radiate a rare warmth of sympathy for sinners, an unquenchable optimism and inextinguishable hope that the worst of human wrecks can be salvaged and sanctified. They have come to know God intimately and recognize Him as omnipotent.

This woman reminds one of the way Clifford Laube once writes of Mary Magdalen, in his poem entitled "Magdalen":

> No art, no ray can re-illume
> A wilted water-lily's bloom;
>
> Nor any alchemy reclaim
> A once-extinguished flame.
>
> Yet innocence, by Heaven's grace,
> Shone again in Mary's face.*

It can shine again in every face no matter what the guilt or the depth of shame. That it should shine is God's will for every ordinary man and woman. That is why what many call the "wrath of God" is often found to be His tender mercy.

Unquestionably we are often, one might say we are *always,* faced with the problem of reconciling what look like contradictories: the goodness of God our Father and the palpable wrongs committed by men which influence the whole course of our lives here on earth, seemingly for the worse. To reconcile these two we have to *think* — something most of us feel a repugnance to doing and always find somewhat difficult. We have to think about reality and consider ultimates. If there is a God He must be sovereign. If He is sovereign these evils perpetrated by men fall under His providence. If that providence of His is personal for me and truly paternal, it must be filled with love. There is only one conclusion allowable: these seeming evils must in some way be good — and even very good for me.

If that bit of philosophizing will not satisfy, then let us turn theologians. There is a book in the Bible which G. K. Chesterton called "one of the four pillars of the universe." Our human existence on this tiny planet is madness unless the Book of Job speaks to our minds and hearts. What does that book tell us? That God *is* God; that everything and everyone, literally everything and everyone, is in the hollow of His hands; that nothing, absolutely nothing, from

---

* From *Crags* (New York: The Monastine Press, 1938). By permission.

the winking of a baby's eye to the explosion of nebulae, comes to pass but by His Will and thanks to His power; that the communists of today, just as the Assyrians in the days of Osee, are working for God and cleansing His people; that earthquakes and tidal waves, hurricanes and tornadoes are all parts of His all-wise and love-filled plan for our good. Job can teach us all common sense that will turn to worship.

One thing the very opening lines of the Book of Job teaches is one thing we ordinary mortals too often forget: namely, that Satan is not God; that the devil is not all-powerful; that over him and all his demons is our Father, without whose permission Satan is utterly powerless, cannot so much as come near us.

Every thinking man will admit that Satan has been granted exceptional latitude in our day. But, unlike the case of Job, the freedom granted him today is due to our *lack* of "simplicity, fear of God, uprightness and avoidance of evil" (Job 1:1). Pius XI, before World War II, told us in more than one encyclical that if we did not turn to prayer and penance God would be forced to let Satan loose. Mother Mary at Fatima, toward the end of World War I, intimated the same when she gave us the formula for survival: prayer and penance. We did not pray. We do not practice penance. What can we expect?

But the point now is that God only *permits* this Satanic latitude. He does not will it! He permits communism. He does not will it. He permits world-wide persecution of His Church. He does not will it. So what He permits we are to face — and fight. He permits moral evil. We are to face it — and fight it. He permits each of us to be tempted. We are to face temptation — and fight it. He permits sickness and myriad sufferings. It is not His Will that we supinely submit to all, but that once we have recognized His hand in these visitations, we then gladly accept the situation and use all the means He has placed at our disposal for the righting of what is wrong. When we have done our utmost and seemingly failed, then we can smile and say *Fiat*. For we can be sure that it is God's Will for us right *now*. We can smile; for we are positive that God is Love and, consequently, nothing will come to us but what is ultimately lovely and lovable. Job teaches you all that — and more.

Get the situation clearly: on the part of man there will be much to blame. Lenin, Stalin, Khrushchev are not likely candidates for canonization. But that does not mean they have not been, and are not *now,* instruments in the hand of God for our good! A surgeon operating on his own child will first render that child unconscious. Now that is not a very nice thing to do to anyone. He will then take a razor-sharp scalpel and deliberately inflict wounds on that child which could kill. Finally, he will cut away even parts of his own child's body — that the child might live. That father is showing his love. We are God's children — and God is Love.

So once we have seen that men can be wrong — and too often are! — we can go on and see that God cannot fail to be right no matter how wrong things appear. One French writer, Father Desurmont, insists that on the part of God and His providence

> everything is just, everything is wise, everything right and good, everything directed to a laudable end, everything brought to a final result which is always absolutely and infinitely amiable. Nero was a monster, still he made martyrs. Diocletian carried the rage of persecution to its uttermost limits, but he thereby prepared for the reaction, and for the triumph of Constantine. Arius was a demon incarnate who would rob Jesus Christ of His Divinity, but it is to his impious efforts that we owe the Church's definitions on this subject. The Barbarians flung themselves on the old world and deluged it with blood, but gave rise to a new race well disposed for Christianity. The Crusades seemed a failure because they did not result in the rescue of Jerusalem, but they were the means of saving Europe. The French Revolution turned everything upside down, but it forced society in self-defense to a renewal of life and vigour.

He is but saying with examples what St. Augustine stated as a principle, namely, that God would never permit evil if He could not draw good from it.

Of course it is not always clear to our very limited intelligence just why God does permit certain evils; nor can we always see what good He draws or has drawn from many He has already allowed. Yet the fact remains that God never makes a mistake, and it is necessary to remind ourselves frequently that we are His children. Many a child has been puzzled by the actions of its loving parents.

Why they will not allow him to do this or that, go with this companion or that, see this show or place or that one, read this book or that, and so on. Nor does the child always understand why these same loving parents insist upon his doing this repugnant thing, going to this unattractive place or with that unprepossessing person. The parents know – and that is enough. So with our Parent, God. He knows what is best for us – and His love will prompt Him to prepare nothing less, if we will be but obedient children.

The sin of our day which has brought so much unhappiness and confusion is the refusal to accept. There is that all-important word again – the refusal to accept God's plan for each of us. The refusal, in other words, to seek to know, and, once known, to do God's Will from this moment to the next. Confusion comes precisely from the presence of so much physical and mental pain in the world. Pagans and many a pagan-minded Christian are literally bewildered by the omnipresence of pain. It seems so purposeless. It is always so unpleasant. In such a milieu we need to know, with a knowledge that is dynamic and life-directing, just precisely what the Book of Job teaches so clearly and what the life of Christ dramatized so convincingly.

"If we have received good things at the hand of God," says Job, "why should we not receive evil?" (Job 2:10.) Earlier, after hearing that all his servants had been slain, his sheep and shepherds destroyed by lightning, his camels taken by Chaldeans, and his seven sons and three daughters killed in "the house of their elder brother" when a "violent wind came," Job simply said: "the Lord gave, and the Lord hath taken away: as it hath pleased the Lord, so is it done: blessed be the name of the Lord" (Job 1:21).

On the basis of that exhibition and on the example of Christ some have urged us Christians to bear all evil with equanimity, and even with joy, not for the hope of reward, but simply because it is the Will of God. That is high spirituality; so high it may well induce vertigo in most of us. But God is God – and merits nothing but adoring obedience from rational creatures. Hence it is comforting to find Paul telling us that Christ Himself "in view of the *joy offered him,* underwent crucifixion with contempt of its disgrace" (Hebr. 12:2). So we need not worry about the "selfishness" in our motives of accepting what God wills in our regard in the line of pain, suffering — and even death.

However, the truth we must never forget, and the one told so fiercely and fully by Job, is that there is only one evil under the sun — and that is not loss of fortune or fame; not loss of friends or family; not loss of position or power; not loss of health or even of earthly life itself. No, Job says with clarion clarity: there is only one loss that can be called evil — and that is the loss of grace. Sin is the only evil under the sun. When will we Christians learn this?

Matthew gives Christ's Sermon on the Mount to us as if it were the first of Christ's public life. His opening words stagger us: "Blessed are the humble souls, for theirs is the kingdom of Heaven." Blessedness, that is, true happiness, which is rooted in and rises from God, is the whole purpose of our striving. We want to be happy with a happiness that will last forever. We can never be that happy until we are lost in God. That, precisely, is what we mean by the "kingdom of Heaven." But to whom does Jesus, the Lamp of heaven, the substantial joy of heaven, promise this Kingdom? — The humble souls! Fathers Kleist and Lilly tell us that the Greek word for "humble" means those of "low rank in life, the downtrodden and oppressed those whom the worldly world looks down upon as mean, despicable; just the type, they say, St. Paul spoke of in his first epistle to the Corinthians when he said: ". . . not many of you were wise . . . influential . . . noble by worldly standards. But God chose what the world holds weak . . . ignoble and despicable, and what counts for nought . . ." (1:26–28).

Christ goes on with ever more astonishing statements, each of which begins with that all-important word "blessed." All our worldly concepts are annihilated as we hear the meek, the gentle, the sorrowing, the hungry and thirsty, the merciful and the single-minded called blessed. But the convulsing climax comes in that last beatitude which tells us that when we are "reviled, or persecuted, or made a target for nothing but malicious lies" for Christ's sake — then we are to "Rejoice; yea, leap for joy . . ." (Mt. 5:3–12).

How many of us do? How many of us really believe the "beatitudes"? Do we allow that word, which is as deep as God, nothing but a "surface existence" and a mere "tinkle of sound"?

When will we "children of light" manifest some wisdom? Of the so-called successful we ask leads, tips, advice, techniques. Of the man who has accumulated a fortune, we ask: "How did you do it?" Of the one who has managed to climb to the top of the political ladder, we ask: "What are the steps?" Of the powerful we ask: "What is the secret?" — But of the only real successes, the saints, what do we ask? When a member of the Society of Jesus asked its founder, St. Ignatius, what the shortest and surest path to perfection and paradise was, he got the reply: "The endurance of many great adversities for the love of Jesus Christ." Father Baltasar Alvarez, a saintly priest of the same Society, said that "sufferings are the post-horses which God sends to us to carry us to Himself speedily. They are the ladder which God offers us so that we may mount to the very heights of perfection. . . . Afflictions, which fall on us like showers of hailstones, are really showers of gold for the soul who is truly patient; for under them the soul gains infinitely more than what she loses." He daringly concludes: "Heaven is the home of the tempted, the afflicted, the despised."

St. Alphonsus, founder of the Redemptorists, once wrote: "Certain people imagine that they are especially beloved by God when everything goes well with them and they have nothing to suffer. Such people labor under a delusion; for it is by adversity, not by prosperity, that God proves the fidelity of His servants, and separates the wheat from the chaff."

Some may misunderstand the saint and think he means that prosperity does not come from God, and is never given His friends. This is not so. Prosperity, success, real triumph come from God every bit as much as defeat, failure, and adversity. Like our earthly fathers, God is glad to make us happy. But like our earthly fathers again, He well knows that few of us can stand perpetual success. As St. Francis de Sales remarked: "Prosperity imperceptibly brings about in us a change of disposition so that we begin to attach ourselves to the gifts and forget the Giver." Let any ordinary man examine himself and honestly answer the question: When did you turn to God with the greater earnestness and know the closer intimacy — was it when enjoying unalloyed success or when you were facing adversity?

Some spiritual writers have asserted that there is no short cut to sanctity. There are saints, however, the truly successful men of earth, who say differently. St. Alphonsus, for one, said: "The science of the saints consist in suffering constantly for Jesus Christ": this is a short cut to sanctification. St. Ignatius of Loyola said: "There is nothing so well calculated to produce and preserve in us the love of God as the wood of the cross." St. Catherine of Genoa considered sickness, temptation, and all such trials indispensable. Blessed Henry Suso once exclaimed: "I am very much afraid God has forsaken me: I have had nothing to suffer from anybody for four weeks. I must be going to the bad."

These men and women knew what they were talking about. So should we — if we would only think! Hasn't every blessing that has been given us in life been given in the form of the cross? Were we not baptized in the form of a cross, given absolution under the sign of a cross? Were we not confirmed and made soldiers of Christ under the form of a cross? In that miracle of all miracles, that daily and even hourly representation of Golgotha and all that it means to God and man, called the Mass, how many signs of the cross can we see! Then when we are fed with God under the appearances of bread and wine, does not the priest give us Christ's Body and Blood, Humanity and Divinity under the form of a cross? When man and woman become channels of grace to one another in the Sacrament of Matrimony does not the Church's official witness, the priest, sign that solemnity with the sign of the cross? Then to make man more than man, to turn him into what St. Ireneus has called a *terrenus deus* — "a God on earth," "a God out of the earthy," "a priest out of a mere man" — some bishop must call down the Holy Spirit and make countless signs of the cross over the aspirant. When sickness has sapped our strength, how does the priest administer those wondrous anointings of the gateways of our senses save in the form of a cross? So from real birth to Christian burial it is always the sign of the cross that brings us blessings God alone can grant. When will we see, then, that every "cross" — every affliction — is really a blessing from God?

Let us continue to call every trial a "cross" only so long as we remember that the cross means salvation! *In hoc signo vinces* — "In this sign thou shalt conquer" — is the legend Constantine saw in the skies when he was battling for world supremacy. We are to recall that legend every time we are asked by God to bear some affliction — to carry some "cross." For actually it is in that sign alone that we shall conquer all that we must conquer if we are to do the Will of God every instant of our lives. Under that sign we can conquer the world's only real evil — sin. Under it we can rout the only real enemy we have in this world — Satan. Under it we can make a friend out of our nearest adversary — our lower self.

Cardinal Merry del Val was wise with the very wisdom of the Son of God when he said: "Let us learn to love the cross, to accept it as our heritage, and as the norm of our life." That sounds almost sadistic until we remember he has but paraphrased what God's only Son stipulated as absolutely necessary in any and all who would be His disciple: "If anyone wants to be my follower," said Christ, "he must renounce himself and shoulder his cross day by day; then he may be a follower of mine" (Lk. 9:23).

It was this same Cardinal Merry del Val, the saintly secretary of state for St. Pius X, who urged his friends to "draw profit from everything that happens, because it comes with the permission and according to the will of the Heart of God." He later said: "Let us have confidence. God will direct all for the best. We see only one page of the great book which He has written for us. He knows all. He can do everything. He loves us. *Fiat!*"

Another cardinal, Mercier of Belgium, once wrote:

> I am going to reveal to you a secret of sanctity and happiness. If every day during five minutes, you will keep your imagination quiet, shut your eyes to all the things of sense, and close your ears to all the sounds of earth, so as to be able to withdraw into the sanctuary of your baptised soul, which is the temple of the Holy Spirit, and speak to that Holy Spirit saying: "I adore Thee, O Holy Spirit. . . . Enlighten, guide, strengthen, and console me. Tell me what I ought to do and command me to do it. I promise to be submissive in everything Thou permittest to happen to me, only show me what is Thy will."
>
> If you do this [says the Cardinal], your life will pass happily and serenely. Consolation will abound even in the midst of troubles. Grace

> will be given in proportion to the trial, as well as strength to bear it, bringing you to the Gates of Paradise full of merit. This submission to the Holy Spirit is the secret of sanctity.

You see this wise and holy man has said in other words what you have been thinking about throughout these long chapters: the Will of God. There is your peace, your happiness, your joy, your sanctification in time and for eternity.

These princes of the Church remind us that "there is no Christianity without tears." They give us no watered-down, maudlin Gospel of Christ. They are actually saying in the present what Paul said so long ago when he wrote to the Galatians: "God forbid that I should glory except in the cross of our Lord Jesus Christ" (Gal. 6:14).

These men present us with no sentimental Christ; for they were men who wanted no sentimental Christians. If ever the world needed red-blooded, full-blooded, fiery-blooded followers of Christ, it needs them now. The second half of the twentieth century is shaped only for men of steel. Christianity is not in danger, for God is still God and faithful to His promises. The gates of hell shall not prevail. But too many Christians are in very grave danger; for they are not intent upon the one thing necessary: the Will of God in their regard *now*. For such, Paul's words ring out with disturbing directness: "As I have often said to you, and now repeat with tears, there are many who conduct themselves as enemies of the cross of Christ. Their end is ruin, their god is their belly, their glory is in their shame, they are earthly minded" (Phil. 3:18–19).

Once again it is necessary to say that "*now* is the acceptable time" and explain that saying by asserting that if you insist on awaiting the day and the hour of the Christ-sized cross; if you persist in biding your time until faced with the all-out challenge of life and love; if you refuse the splinters and even the mere shadow of Christ's cross, looking for the moment when you will be called upon for that heroic sacrifice which will spell your sanctification, you will never become a saint, your life will never be a success. You must start *now,* with the cross at hand, even though it be but a splinter, and bear it gladly for God, simply because it is His Will for you.

Do that from hour to hour, day to day, and you have already arrived.

Ronald Knox, when leaving his Anglican friends for the Catholic Church, parted by wishing each of them: "The greatest of God's earthly blessings: the consciousness of doing His will."* That blessing can be yours now – and always. Take up the cross He holds out to you *now*.

"Do not look forward to what might happen tomorrow," says St. Francis de Sales. "The same Everlasting Father who cares for you today will take care of you tomorrow and every day. Either He will shield you from suffering or he will give you unfailing strength to bear it. Be at peace, then, and put aside all anxious thoughts and imaginations."

The secret of the imperturbability of the saints lies in their acceptance of the *now* – with all that it contains – as the full revelation of God for them personally. Since the moment is filled with God, it is overflowing with love. How could they be other than happy and filled with peace?

Just as we have insisted that Christianity is not a cult of suffering but a Religion of joy – and a Religion that gives joy now as well as in eternity – we must here insist that it is not suffering that spells sanctity, but only suffering accepted (That word again!) and accepted as the Will of God. That lesson was taught unforgettably on Calvary where "three men shared death . . . but only one man died!" Are you going to be like that one man, or will you be as wise as the Good Thief and turn your cross into a key to heaven? You see that it can be done; for already it has been done by man.

Now is the time; for tomorrow never comes. Or better still: "tomorrow we die."

---

* *Spiritual Aeneid,* p. 217.

CHAPTER ELEVEN

THE FINAL NOW... IS JOY-FILLED AND UNENDING

Some ordinary men and women are no doubt destined to go through life without experiencing physical suffering or agonizing bodily sickness. It may even be that it is God's Will for them to live on earth without any real mental pain or deep moral anguish. But for every son of Adam and daughter of Eve there is one certainty: he and she will face a final *now*. Abel was the first human being to know death. From then until time's last tick, no matter what else human beings have managed to escape or may yet be able to avoid, no one of them will ever manage to escape death. You will face it. How will you meet it?

This final moment merits much attention. It is the most important of all the many moments God grants us. On the way we measure up to it depends our state in that now which will never end – the now of eternity.

Someone has said that "Courage is only fear that has said its prayers." If that be true, then it would seem that not many of us have said our prayers on this matter of death. For if there is one word most people shrink from even using it is "death." Yet we read how St. Paul *longed* for it. St. Thérèse of the Child Jesus, when on her deathbed, was asked if she was resigned to die. "Ah, Father," this child of God replied, "I find that it is only to live that one has need of resignation. Death will be a joy to me."

The ordinary man will say: "That is all very well for a saint; but for us . . ." But let every ordinary man and woman stop right there; for we have faced and accepted the conclusion that no man or woman has any other reason for being on earth than to become a saint. Then there is the fact that it is God's Will that we all should die — and, now, there is nothing else we want to do in heaven or on earth but His Will.

Not so long ago there was a man in Death Row of Kentucky's State Prison at Eddyville. He had confessed that at one time "God was only a three-letter word to him, and that, as far as any practical bearing on his life was concerned, those three letters might just as well have been x y z." Yet, when the warden of the prison entered his cell at six o'clock February 25, 1943, to read the death warrant, Tom Penney stood up and listened quietly. That warrant said that he was to die that night at midnight, since he had been found guilty of the robbery in which two women were killed. When the warden finished reading, Penney bowed his head in a gracious nod and said, "Thank you, Mr. Buchanan. God's holy Will be done. I am a lucky man."

No one will ever place Tom Penney in the same category with Saul of Tarsus or Thérèse of Lisieux; yet it would seem that we can place him beside the so-called "Good Thief" — St. Dismas, the man who stole heaven with his last moment. What is more, when one examines the letters Penney wrote on his last day on earth, one can find sentiments very similar to those of St. Paul. For Tom Penney wrote to Father Brian, a Passionist who had given a mission to the men in Eddyville: "I am feeling fine, Father. . . . The love of God is so strongly embedded in my heart that knowledge of the 'inevitable' has brought a resignation to me that makes the prospect pleasing, yes, even joyfully so. My love of God still outweighs my love of life. I seek not the consolation of God, but the God of consolations; not the gift, but the Giver. . . ." To another Passionist, who had advised him by letters, he wrote: "Let it be some measure of comfort to you to know that you have helped me with your wonderful letters of advice and encouragement. Without them I might not now be able to say with the great Apostle: 'I have fought the good fight, and I have kept the Faith.' . . . At last the time has come to say 'Good bye' — but I won't say it. I'll say instead: 'Until we meet in Heaven!' . . ."

This man is the one who had said "God is only a three-letter word to me. . . ." He was an accomplice in a robbery in which two murders were committed. Yet, on his last day on earth and as his final moment neared he wrote to his mother and family: "I implore you, give thanks, *everlasting* thanks to the good God who is present in my heart, for giving me the grace to die a happy death. Keep your chins up. . . . I'll be watching and waiting to greet you – do not let me down."

This man had his finger on the pulse of reality. The word "death" did not frighten him. Yet he had lived a life that was anything but that of a saint. How explain such a metamorphosis? *Metanoia* is the word. He had undergone a real conversion. He had come to know the God who had permitted him to sin but whose will was his sanctification. To Father George Donnelly, the priest who had instructed him, he wrote on this final day:

> . . . I had counted heavily on your being here tonight, Father, and thought I could tell you my appreciation personally, but it seems that our Lord has ordained otherwise, so now I am out on a limb. How can I write all those things I want to say? I have no secrets from you, Father, unless it is that I have kept you in ignorance of the miracle that God has wrought in my soul. . . . Five more hours, dear Father, and I will meet our Lord and our Lady with all the Holy Saints and Angels. Bet your socks you'll get talked about. . . ."

Who can question what was the most joy-filled *now* of this man's life? Should the final one be any different for any man or woman? Just gaze, as Tom Penney did, at what lies ahead: the vision of God, the face of Christ in glory, the loveliness of Mary Immaculate our Mother, the rapture of the encounter with Michael, Raphael, Gabriel, and the unfolding of the splendor of the full nine choirs of angels. Think of meeting your own guardian angel who has been with you every split second of the way. Dwell on the joy of seeing your patron saints; of looking upon the faces of Peter and of Paul; of listening to Augustine, Aquinas, Bonaventure, and Bernard; of chatting with the patriarchs, the prophets, the judges, and kings of the Old Testament and of holding converse with the Fathers of the Church – both those of the East and those of the West. . . .

Is that all too heady? Then think on something even closer to the heart. Father Frank O'Boyle, S.J., had lived a long, studious, and very laborious life. His final now found him physically helpless in a bed in St. Joseph Infirmary, Louisville, Kentucky. As a fellow priest bent over him to say: "Soon, Father dear, you'll be going to heaven . . ." the weak, white head turned, luminous eyes grew bright, and in a wavering voice that held smiles in every syllable he said: "Yes, and I know there are many friends waiting up there for me."

Tertullian once asked: "Why do we fear that which ends all fears?" Can we not parallel him and ask: "Why don't we long for, and love more, that which will satisfy all our longings and give us all we love?"

If we focus on the physical aspect of death, it is not a thing of beauty. It is a punishment laid upon us by God for sin. Punishments are never beautiful. Then there is the separation of those two substances that were never meant to be separated. God never planned that human soul should be torn from human body by that agonizing rending which men call death. Had Adam obeyed, Eve would never have been bewildered by the sight of her boy's lifeless body after Cain had murdered him, nor would our world have been turned into one huge graveyard. Death in itself, and more particularly in its physical aspect, is anything but appealing. Yet for the true member of Christ, for the man or woman who has become conscious of life's greatest reality, that physical aspect is despised just as Christ, our Head, despised the shame of the cross "in view of the joy offered . . ." (Hebr. 12:2).

Certain as the last now for each of us is, it is crowded with uncertainties. We know not the day — nor the hour . . . we know not whether we will be surrounded by friends or strangers, or whether we will be entirely alone . . . we know not where nor under what circumstances. . . .

An eminent Kentucky surgeon began the First Friday, which is, in a way, always a feast of the Sacred Heart, in the month of June, which is the month of the Sacred Heart, as he had opened almost every other day of his adult life: by assisting at Mass in company with his beloved wife. At Communion time this particular First Friday, he stepped out of the pew and drew back, as usual, to allow Mrs. Henry to precede him to the rail. When she arrived there she was surprised to note that the doctor did not kneel beside her. They had compacted to receive God in the Blessed Sacrament side by side whenever possible, so this failure on the doctor's part distracted her for a moment. But only for a moment. For immediately she was absorbed in God. But as she made her way back to her place she was shaken out of her absorption by a small knot of people which had gathered there, bending over the form of a man. It was her husband. One look told her that instead of her Joseph receiving God that morning, God had received him. Doctor Henry's last now on earth was fitting prelude to his unending now in heaven. The Author of time had split the darkness of time with the radiance of eternity for a man who had ever been approaching Him who is Light and the Lamp of heaven. There was no death struggle to speak of; surely there was no death agony. Holy Communion, to which he was ready to go, became heavenly union as the Sacred Heart stopped the beating of the doctor's human heart. Through "heart failure" Doctor Henry knew his heart's fulfillment. The only way to such fulfillment is through what men call death – and that passage can be painless. Why do we fear?

Father Marion Batson, S.J., had volunteered as a scholastic, to go to India and to spend his life there, asking God to accept this deliberate displacing of himself as sacrifice that would plead for the conversion of his father. In that foreign land he labored for over thirty years. In 1960 he came back to the United States for a few months of recuperation and recruiting work. During those few months God willed that he hold his dying mother in his arms and learn from her lips that, while his father died a holy death, he had not entered the Church's visible body. The priest was not disheartened. He knew that every prayer receives some reply, and was sure that the prayer of his thirty years had not fallen on heedless ears, let alone on an indifferent Heart. So it was with joy that he prepared to go back to India and pray on by a life of labor. A group of friends had gathered with what was left of his family at the Chicago airport the morning he was scheduled to start his long flight back to India. As plane time neared they grew puzzled by the nonappearance of Father Marion. Finally they called the Jesuit house where he had been staying. The reply they received to their inquiry is one that should quiet all foolish fear about death agonies. They were told Father Marion would not be flying back to India, for, while the priest slept, the Christ, whom he had served so generously and in whose Society he had lived so long, had kept His promise. He had "come like a thief in the night."

Another useless fear is that of the devil. So many cringe at the thought that the devil and all his satellites will be around the deathbed. Many accounts of such a happening have come down to us. They are certainly well calculated to instill fear into the most courageous. But only if we refuse to think. The devil and all hell may surround your deathbed *only* if God permits it. Never forget that there is only one God. Satan can do nothing without His permission. And God does not grant that permission except for a holy reason! Hence, if it be God's permissive Will that you be tormented, you can rejoice. The devil never torments those he is sure of! Therefore, if you are actually tormented, it can only mean that so far you are safe. But there is a further thought that is essential. . . .

God made you — not that He might eternally damn you, but that you might glorify Him for all eternity. Once He had called you into being by an act of His omnipotent Will, He had to sustain you in being by a continuing act of that same omnipotent Will. There has never been a breath drawn by you that was not also drawn by God. There has never been a pulse beat in your body that was not set beating by Him. And all for one purpose: that ultimately you might glorify Him by formal glory throughout eternity. Is it at all likely that this all-wise God is going to forsake you in your last now? Once again we plead with you to remember that He and He alone is omnipotent. Compared with His power, Satan and all hell are utter impotence. So what if all hell is around you in your last moment? If God be with you who can be against you — with any deleterious effect?

Think on! God sent His only Son to earth, and as has so well been said, He was sent for *you* — just as if you were the only human being who ever needed to be redeemed by an infinite Being. Think on the humiliations of His thirty-three years — from that conception in the dark womb of a little Jewish maid unto that burial in the dark of Arimathea's borrowed tomb. Think of the measureless anguish of Gethsemani, of the horror and shame of that whipping post, of the piercing pain in every thorn point. Weigh, if you can, the weight of the cross. Hear Him cry from Golgotha: "My God! My God! Why hast Thou forsaken Me?" Watch His head sink in death. Then with Paul say to yourself: "He loved *me!*" Say of yourself: "He delivered Himself up for *me!*" Then ask yourself: "Is it likely that He will abandon me in my last now?" So, if all hell be howling about your deathbed, hear His quiet voice saying: "Have confidence! I have overcome. . . . I am your Head. I have loved you with an everlasting love."

Still think on! From His deathbed He made you a special bequest. As final legacy He left you His Mother to be mother to you. Recall her Seven Sorrows — and remember that seven in Scripture is a number signifying fullness. She, your mother, is Gateway of all grace — and very especially of that final grace no man can merit: the grace of final perseverance! She is the Help of Christians — omnipotent in her power to supplicate! She is Refuge of sinners. She is Queen of the universe. Where will she be, and what will she be doing as you face your final now? Do you know anything of a mother's love? Do you realize to what lengths any mother will go to save her child? Have you ever realized all you mean to Mary — not because of what you are in yourself but precisely for what you are "in Christ Jesus"? You are His member. Hence, as St. Pius X has taught, she held you in her womb spiritually when she held Him there physically. She formed you spiritually then — and all down the years. She is the Woman told of in Genesis, the one who was to crush Satan's head. She is the Woman clothed in the sun, as the Apocalypse details, before whom the mighty dragon was powerless. If Michael could drive Satan into hell, what can this Queen of the angels do to him? She is your hope — how can you fear?

Run down the Litany of the Saints, realizing all the while that each is more interested in your soul and its salvation than you are; for they know, as you cannot now know, just how precious that soul is to their Queen, to their Lord, to their God. That is the Litany said for the dying. It is a cry to them to come; a cry they never fail to hear and answer.

So if God should permit all hell to surround you at your last moments — what a weakness would be pitted against your lovers and your determined, God-filled defenders!

Look into your own soul. If you see aright, all fear will vanish. For that soul has a gravitational pull toward God. In your final now that pull will exert its greatest force. One wonders sometimes if this springing back to its Source by the soul is not the very essence of that thing called death.

With every throb of your heart, then, hear Christ saying: "Fear not! I have overcome. . . ."

The nagging doubt still persists: "Granted that all this is true, it still remains a question whether I can really take this onslaught."

That is not a question. It should not be a doubt. For it is a certainty that *you* cannot take it. That is, you as you — as a mere human being. But you ceased to be you and a mere human being when you were baptized. You then became His member — and it is the Person who acts and suffers in and through the body. *Actiones et passiones sunt suppositorum* say the philosophers; meaning that when your hand or foot strikes an object, it is not your hand or your foot that receives the credit or the blame, it is you. When you suffer from a headache, it is not your head that aches, but you who ache in your head. So in Christ's Mystical Body. You will not suffer any death agony alone. It will be Christ in you and you in Christ. Without Him you can do nothing worthwhile for eternity. But "in Him, and through Him, and with Him," you will conquer!

So no matter the circumstances of your last moment, it is a moment charged and even surcharged with God. That makes it, no matter what its appearances, the grandest now of all the nows of time. If it be overflowing with suffering, rejoice; for as Dante wisely said: "suffering remarries us to God."

Teresa of Avila certainly loved God and longed to be with Him; yet she tells us in her autobiography that she would willingly suffer unto the end of time if by doing so she could increase God's glory one degree. "Either let me suffer, Lord," she prayed, "or let me die." Her aged friend, María Díaz, when asked in her eightieth year if she were not longing to go home to heaven replied: "On the contrary, my desire is to enter heaven as late as possible. For so long as I am on earth, I can offer my God something I will not be able to offer Him in heaven – my sufferings." So you see there is nothing to fear in our last now, no matter what its allotment be.

Ignatius of Loyola advises indifference to a long life or a short life. Both have advantages. Both have disadvantages. Leave all to the Will of God in His directive, and love only that. The same with wealth or poverty, fame or infamy, health or sickness. Leave all to the Will of God. What He gives will be best for each of us. St. Francis de Sales summed this directive up neatly in his maxim: "Desire nothing, ask for nothing, refuse nothing." He lived that maxim out to the very end; for when his friends urged him to repeat the prayer of St. Martin who when dying said: "Lord, if I am still necessary to Thy people, I refuse not the labor," St. Francis replied: "I'll do nothing of the sort. I charge myself with the care of leading a good life. The care of my death I abandon to God."

Wise man indeed. For "as we live, so shall we die; and as we die, so shall we live for all eternity." If we live from *now* to the next *now* striving to do God's Will we will die doing just that and nothing else. For let us never forget Paul's words to Timothy: "God wills that all men be saved and come to the knowledge of the truth" (1 Tim. 2:4). Join them to those words of Christ: "This is the sum of eternal life – their knowing you, the only true God, and your ambassador Jesus Christ" (Jn. 17:3).

Do that every day and you will be very like Leon Bloy when your last now comes. As this ardent lover of God lay dying, a friend bent over and asked: "What are you experiencing, Leon?" and received the reply: "A consuming curiosity." He was looking ahead. He was straining to see God. He was feeling that body-rending pull of the soul toward its Source. He was aflame with a curiosity that was holy desire.

Here in Kentucky this past year a woman died who looked back over a lifetime of illness and saw God's hand upon her every step of the way. She had undergone twenty-two surgical operations and had spent seven years in bed because of tuberculosis; when she finally was allowed up, almost every known disease seemed to attack her. For twenty years she was able to leave her house only once. "I did not enjoy sickness, nor suffering, nor the nervous agony and exhaustion that are harder to bear than physical pain," she wrote just before death. "And an invalid has to bury many dear dreams that have death struggles and refuse to die decently and quietly. But God has a way of taking away our toys, and after we have cried for a while like disappointed children, He fills our hands with jewels. . . ."

Among the greatest of those jewels was what she called "the peace of God that would sink into my soul. When it came I would see that, after all, it mattered little that my broken body suffered, since the body's loss must be the spirit's gain. I saw further that nothing that happens to us is important save insofar as it affects our spiritual development, our knowledge of God, and our growth in faith."

Then she went on to say that

> we sick people have so much leisure! Unwelcome some times, but blessed beyond measure when rightly used. God's voice is a still, small voice, and we must listen well in order to hear it. At times we can only feel Him, and rest quietly beneath His hand. Of course one of the hardest things about being sick is a feeling of uselessness. We want to work for God. Oh, indeed, it is good to work for God, but it is better just to do His Will, and evidently it is His Will that not all should work. Some day He will tell us about that.
>
> But there is one great ministry in which even we sick ones may share, and I thank God for that, the ministry of prayer. It is a marvelous, a breathtaking thought that I, lying here on my bed in my small room, may help set in operation the vast machinery of God, may change the destiny of a life, a world, may even hasten the day of His appearing!

Remember this is from the pen of a woman who lived in the world. It is not the writing of a nun. She goes on to say

> After I had been sick for several years, I thought in my foolishness, that I had learned the lessons God had wanted to teach me, and that now He would let me go out into the world and work for Him. As if one could ever learn all God has to teach! No, I am still sick. I do not understand why I must still be an invalid. I no longer expect to understand. If I did, there would be no need of faith. Enough that He knows why—and some day He will tell me why it was best for me and best for His cause.
>
> Then came the hardest blow of all: nearly nine years ago He

> called my beloved husband and left me here alone, crippled with arthritis, facing cancer, with dimming eyesight and other illnesses. . . . Then, indeed, I learned about God and how His strength is made perfect in weakness, and how He can supply all my needs "according to his riches in glory in Christ Jesus" (Phil. 4:19). It is one thing to think so – it is another thing to have found out by actual experience that it is so, to know beyond a shadow of a doubt that when you go down into the valley, you can clasp His hand – that you never need be alone nor afraid; for He will go with you on all paths, and His arm is strong enough to carry you. It is blessed beyond words to *know* these things.

It is obvious that in this woman Dante's words are realized: sorrow and suffering had remarried her to God. Sickness and the death of her loved one were priceless blessings. Yet there was a greater gift which she finally discovered. This is how she described it:

> The best part of it all is the blessed hope of His coming soon. How I ever lived before I grasped this truth, I do not know. How anyone can live without it in these trying days, I cannot imagine. Each morning I think with a leap of my heart: "Today, He may come!" Each evening I say to myself: "When I awake, I may be in glory." Thus I live each day as if it were to be my last. I am on tiptoe with expectancy. There are no more gray days – for they are all touched with His color; no more dark days – for the radiance of His coming is on the horizon; no more dull days – with glory just around the corner; and no more lonely days – with His footstep coming ever nearer, and the thought that soon, soon I shall see His Face!

Should you begin or end your ordinary day any other way than did this eloquent woman? Should you not now be able to say what she said at the end of this remarkable confession: "The main thing, of course, which my illness has brought me is a *knowledge of God and of Jesus Christ* 'in whom are hid all the treasures of wisdom and knowledge' " (Col. 2:3). Sickness had given her heaven on earth, eternity in time; for Christ has said: "And this is the sum of eternal life – their knowing you, the only true God, and your ambassador, Jesus Christ" (Jn. 17:3).

There may yet be hardheaded realists who will insist that it is not death we ordinary mortals fear, but the Judgment.

There is truth in that claim of course. For Ecclesiastes tells us that "man knoweth not whether he be worthy of love or hatred" (9:1). That uncertainty makes men uneasy. But once again the plea is: Think! We have a conscience. It's voice can be quite clear. What does it tell you of your state. If you listen, you will learn whether you are standing in the state of God — which we call the state of grace — or whether you are standing over against Christ. In short, while we can never have metaphysical certitude about our state of soul, we can, and we always should have definite moral certitude. And for the thinking man that is enough.

We are going to face the Judge the moment we die. But look at Him! Do you not recognize your Brother? Jesus, who died for you — who lived and died just that you might not die forever — is to be your Judge. Can you fear a Judge whose very essence is love, and whose quintessence, if we may speak this way, is merciful love?

God is just. God is jealous. God is judge. But His very justice and jealousy will make Him merciful. Hence, to the thinking man, death holds no fears; for the thinking man becomes a love-filled man — and as St. John says: "There is no fear in love; rather perfect love drives out fear" (1 Jn. 4:18). The thinking man is filled with that unshakable trust that comes from unquestioning love.

Cardinal Newman was a thinking man. That is why he could write:

> God has created me to do Him some definite service; He has committed some work to me which He has not committed to another. I have my mission — I may never know what it is in this life, but I shall be told it in the next. I am a link in a chain, a bond of connection between persons. He has not created me for naught. I shall do good. I shall do His work. I shall be an angel of peace, a preacher of truth in my own place while not intending it — if I do but keep His Commandments. Therefore, I will trust Him. Whatever, wherever I am, I can never be thrown away. If I am in sickness, my sickness may serve Him; in perplexity, my perplexity may serve Him; if I am in sorrow, my sorrow may serve Him. He does nothing in vain. He knows what He is about. He may take away my friends, He may throw me among strangers. He may make me feel desolate, make my spirits sink, hide my future from me — still He knows what He is about. I will trust Him.

Must not every thinking man and woman say the same right now?

St. Joseph Pignatelli, S.J., has put the whole case for us when he prayed:

> O my God, I know not what must come to me today; but I am certain that nothing can happen to me which Thou hast not foreseen, decreed, and ordained from all eternity. That is enough for me.
>
> I adore Thy impenetrable and eternal designs, to which I submit with all my heart. I desire, I accept them all, and unite my sacrifice to that of Jesus Christ, my Saviour. I ask in His name, and through His infinite merits, patience in trials, and perfect submission to all that comes to me through Thy Holy Will. Amen.

There is the prayer for every day and every hour of the day. If lived, our final now will be what it should be: joy-filled and glorious.

But to return to the thought with which we began: we have only the present, passing *now*. Why be absorbed by one that has not yet come and may not? This present *now* can be our last. Live it to the hilt of its holiness by taking it from God and for God, accepting all it holds as His manifestation of love and trust in us, returning it to Him as the good servants returned the talents: doubled!

We receive God's Will only in fragments; tiny fragments; one to each new now. It is our business to take them and piece them together, to fashion them into the design that is His and has been His from all eternity. What that design is we shall see only at our last moment. It will be perfect as God wills it to be perfect only if we live His Will in the now, the only fragment of time that is ours, the only fragment of God's plan that is allowed in our hands, the only fragment of Christ's life in us and our life in Christ that can be lived. But it is only by "gathering up these fragments, lest they be lost" that we can really live and attain to life's only success — sainthood.

This may all appear too easy. But never forget that this is addressed to those who want to do God's Will from *now* to *now*. For them the thesis has been and still is that sanctity is easy; inasmuch as sanctity is simple; it is increased from moment to moment, day to day, year to year in those who live only in the present and doing therein God's Will for them — the duty of the present moment for their state of life. Such people live a life of love in Christ Jesus and as Jesus Christ; for they are ever conscious that they are His members with a work to do: the same that He had to do when He was on earth: the Will of the Father! These people overcome — just as Christ overcame — the world, the flesh, and the devil. To these have been given those magnificent promises of the Apocalypse: "Be faithful unto death, and I will give thee the crown of life" (Apoc. 2:11). "To him who overcomes . . . I will give authority over the nations. And he shall rule them with a rod of iron . . . and I will give him the morning star" (Apoc. 2:26–28). "He who overcomes shall be arrayed thus in white garments . . . and I will confess his name before my Father, and before his Angels" (Apoc. 3:5). "He who overcomes, I will make a pillar in the temple of my God . . . and I will write upon him the name of my God, and the name of the city of my God . . . and my new name" (Apoc. 3:12–13). "He who overcomes, I will permit him to sit with me upon my throne . . ." (Apoc. 3:21).

God the Holy Spirit throughout these revelations promises you and me that triumph of all triumphs: endless union "in Christ Jesus, through Christ Jesus, and with Christ Jesus" with the Father and the Spirit for all eternity. Small wonder that John ended this book with the cry: "Come, Lord Jesus!"

And that will be our cry in our last now if we live always as members of Christ. Then our last heartbeats will be but a praying of that prayer of all prayers: "Our Father, who art in Heaven, hallowed be Thy name, Thy Kingdom come, Thy will be done" — in me — *now!*